BEYOND THE VERSE

WHAT I DISCOVERED READING THE BIBLE ONE BOOK AT A TIME

Wes McAdams

Copyright © 2019 Wes McAdams

Beyond the Verse: What I Discovered Reading the Bible One Book at a Time

All rights reserved. No part of this book may be reproduced in any form or by any electronic or mechanical means including information storage and retrieval systems, without permission in writing from the author. The only exception is by a reviewer, who may quote short excerpts in a review.

A "Radically Christian" Book.

Visit the blog at RadicallyChristian.com

Unless otherwise indicated, Scripture quotations are from The ESV® Bible (The Holy Bible, English Standard Version®), copyright © 2001 by Crossway, a publishing ministry of Good News Publishers. Used by permission. All rights reserved.

Dedicated to my father, Weldon McAdams, who has been one of the greatest examples of Christian growth and transformation I have ever witnessed. He taught me, if you are not growing, you are dying.

CONTENTS

INTRODUCTION 1
GENESIS 5
EXODUS 8
LEVITICUS 11
NUMBERS 13
DEUTERONOMY 16
JOSHUA 19
JUDGES 22
SAMUEL 25
KINGS 28
ISAIAH 32
JEREMIAH 35
EZEKIEL 38
MINOR PROPHETS 41
JOB 45
PROVERBS 48
RUTH 51
SONG OF SOLOMON 54
ECCLESIASTES 57
LAMENTATIONS 60
ESTHER 63
DANIEL 66

EZRA-NEHEMIAH	69
CHRONICLES	72
CONNECTING THE TESTAMENTS	75
MATTHEW	78
MARK	82
LUKE	85
JOHN	88
ACTS	91
ROMANS	94
1 CORINTHIANS	98
2 CORINTHIANS	102
GALATIANS	106
EPHESIANS	109
PHILIPPIANS	112
COLOSSIANS	115
THESSALONIANS	118
TIMOTHY & TITUS	121
PHILEMON	125
HEBREWS	128
JAMES	131
1 PETER	134
2 PETER	138
JOHN'S EPISTLES	141
JUDE	144
REVELATION	147

INTRODUCTION

Like many Christians, I used to think of the Bible as a large collection of verses. If a person wanted to know the truth about any given subject, all he or she had to do was find the right verses that spoke to that issue. In other words, the Bible was sort of like a dictionary or an encyclopedia of religious stories and ideas.

As a whole, I believed the Bible was primarily about how to go to heaven and not hell. I once heard someone joke that you could think of the word Bible as an acronym, "B-I-B-L-E, Basic Instructions Before Leaving Earth." Essentially, I believed that was true enough. The Bible was a set of instructions to teach every person how to go to heaven. Some verses were meant to be taken as examples of what to do; others, what not to do; and still others, commands to follow. I really didn't know how else to read it.

Even when I sat down and read several consecutive chapters, I would do so looking for verses that I liked. I would highlight or underline the verse, thinking, *I can use that verse to prove such and such idea.* I wasn't paying attention to what the author of that book was really trying to communicate or how the original audience might have read it; I was looking for ammunition to prove my foregone conclusions.

Somewhere along the way, that all began to change. I slowly started to see I was pulling verses out of their context to make them say what I wanted them to say. I was combining various verses from multiple books to piece together my theology. I thought what I was doing was "systematic theology," but it was really just twisting and distorting the intended message of Scripture.

Reading Whole Books

I began to reason, if a particular book of the Bible was a letter a friend sent me, I wouldn't treat it this way. I wouldn't pull a sentence or two out of context and focus on that. I would read the letter over and over again as a whole.

So I started reading some of the epistles of the New Testament in one sitting. First, I discovered it was not nearly as time consuming or challenging as I thought it would be to sit down and read 4 or 5 chapters. Even reading 16 chapters or so wasn't too bad.

Doing this helped me to see things in these books I had never seen before. I read every verse in the Bible multiple times, but I had never read it like this. But the worst part was discovering there were many verses I had completely misunderstood. The meaning I had assigned to those verses had nothing to do with the author's actual train of thought or the overall message of the book. Realizing this, I wondered what else I had misunderstood about the Bible.

So I decided to read each book of the Bible in one sitting and then summarize my thoughts and conclusions on each book. It took me about 16 months to complete this project, because sometimes it's difficult to find a day to invest 4 hours to sit down and read the longer books. I wasn't always able to read the book without interruptions, but I was able to complete each book in a single day.

This book is the result of that journey through the Bible. But before you dive into my conclusions, there are a few things I need to share with you.

Why I Wrote This Book

I didn't write this book to be the final word, and certainly not a scholarly word, on each book of the Bible. I don't want you to read this book thinking I am trying to tell you what each book of the Bible means. I am not presenting these summaries to you to educate you, but to inspire you.

I want to inspire you to embark on the same sort of journey. I want you to start (or continue) reading whole books of the Bible in a single day. I want you to find a few hours on a Saturday and sit down with the book of Genesis. I want you to wrestle with some of the thoughts I present in each chapter. I just want to be your friend and companion that walks with you through the exciting biblical world.

I want each chapter of this book to whet your appetite and spark your curiosity. I want to start a conversation with you. I'm confident you will discover things I missed and draw deeper and better conclusions than I did. That's the whole point of this book: to move you to action.

The Hebrew Order and Missing Psalms

As you glance through the chapters, you may notice a couple of things. First, I ordered my reading according to the way the Hebrew Bible is ordered. There are some books of the Hebrew Bible that were originally part of one work, so I read and considered those together (e.g. the Minor Prophets). Also, the Hebrew Bible is organized in three parts: Torah, Prophets, and Writings (in Hebrew, that is shortened to "TaNaK"). Consequently, I read and summarized some of the books in a slightly different order than they are found in our English Bibles.

Second, I did not include the book of Psalms because, of all the books in the Bible, Psalms is actually designed to be read, meditated upon, and even sung chapter-by-chapter rather than as an entire collection. It is definitely possible to read through the whole collection of Psalms in a single sitting and I have no doubt it would be beneficial, but it was not something I undertook as part of this process.

Lack of Bible References

You will find that I often include direct quotes from the book under consideration, but I do not include a Scripture reference with my summary. This isn't a mistake or oversight. I did this for two reasons:

First, I don't want to proof-text my way through a summary. I did not conclude what I concluded based on a single verse, but based on the book as a whole. That single verse was simply an illustrative quote that encapsulated the heart and essence of the point the author was making.

Second, I don't want you to cheat. If you're reading my summary and you disagree with what I'm saying, I don't want you to look up that one particular verse and draw your conclusions based on the verse before it and the verse after it, I want you to take your disagreement and go read the whole book. Remember, I am sharing my summaries with you in order to get you to read whole books in a single sitting.

When I quoted passages from outside the book under consideration, I tried to always include a Scripture reference. I wanted you to know in which book you could find that exact quote and also to see how the entirety of Scripture ties together.

How It Relates to Jesus

Finally, when considering each book of the Bible, my primary concern was understanding how it relates to Jesus. I wanted to see, and I wanted you to see, how the over-arching narrative of Scripture leads to Jesus.

So, don't be surprised when even the chapters on the Old Testament end with a discussion of Jesus. For me, it's all about him.

GENESIS

Because many of us have heard and read the stories in Genesis our entire lives, it can be a tricky book to read with fresh eyes. But like the first few minutes of a movie, it's vitally important that we truly understand the book of Genesis in order to understand the books that follow. We cannot simply assume, because we can articulate the flood story or the story of Abraham, that we have a firm grasp on the key themes and elements of the book of Genesis.

So, in order to help you realize there may be some elements we often overlook, I want to share with you seven things I noticed in my reading that I had often overlooked or been unable to articulate. These observations are in no particular order, but they stuck out to me as things that are important, but often overlooked or misunderstood:

1. "Be fruitful and multiply" isn't a command, but a blessing. Fertility is a blessing theme throughout the book.

2. The earth/ground is one of the leading characters in the story.

3. God not only promised to not repeat the flood, he also promised never to curse the ground or strike down all the animals again because of man's sin. We must keep this in mind, because however the story of the Bible ends, it will not end with God breaking this promise.

4. For the patriarchs, one reason having offspring was so important was that they seemed to think of living on through the life of their sons as a form of immortality.

5. With few exceptions, there doesn't seem to be any real reason to think the characters of the story ought to be imitated. The "good guys" are often as foolish and wicked as the "bad guys." So Genesis should not be read as a collection of moral parables.

6. The story has its climax in the life of Joseph. You might think the whole story was about Joseph, except that at the end of the story he dies with an anticipation of God's promises yet to be fulfilled.

7. Burial is important to Joseph and to all of God's people. Not just as a cultural practice, but as a way of anticipating the promises of God yet to be fulfilled.

There are certainly many other things that can and should be said about the book of Genesis, but I hope this list helps give you a pair of fresh eyes to go back to the book and start asking, "What else might I have missed?"

It's Not About How to Go to Heaven

With that being said, the primary thought I had while reading the book was this: Genesis is supposed to be the introduction to a grand narrative, unfolding among the Israelite people for centuries, until it finally culminates in the coming of Jesus. If that is true, then we have to let Genesis set the stage in its own way. We have to let it tell us what kind of a story the Bible is going to be.

The typical Christian seems to believe the Bible is simply an instruction manual for how to go to heaven when they die. But that doesn't seem to be the kind of story Genesis is introducing. There is absolutely nothing in the whole book about going to heaven when we die. And there is also very little in the way of actual instruction within the book. If you gave someone a Bible with the impression that they were supposed to treat this book as a set of instructions for how to go to heaven when they die, they would likely be very confused before they even finished the first, introductory book.

What Story is Being Introduced?

Rather, it seems to me, the story that is being introduced is one in which a good God created a good world. He set mankind up as earth's royal overseers and caretakers. They betrayed God's trust and were condemned to live as exiles. But rather than destroying them, God sympathized with their weakness and set in motion a plan to restore and bless them through the offspring of a man named Abraham.

As it turns out, God's Messiah will be much like Joseph. He will be destined for greatness even from childhood. He will resist temptation. He will be betrayed by his brothers. Though innocent of any crime, he will be condemned, but will be vindicated and raised up alive. He will be crowned with power and authority. He will save both Israel and the Gentiles from death. He will bless and forgive those who betrayed him.

And greatest of all, Abraham and his family will literally be raised from the dead through the coming Messiah. In this way, God will break the curse of sin and death, reconciling all the things of heaven and earth. The hope of the patriarchs, who believed they would live on through their offspring, will literally come to fruition in the Messiah.

That's the story Genesis is setting up. And to me, understanding that makes all the difference as you read the Bible all the way to the end.

EXODUS

There are certainly a lot of things which could be said about the book of Exodus, and there were several things I noticed this time I had not noticed before. However, I consider one element of this book to be of utmost importance.

It's About Slaves

The book of Exodus is the story of how a faithful God heard the cries of an oppressed group of slaves and rescued them in order to crown them with glory and honor, make them a holy people, and dwell in their midst.

Think about it. Of all the people groups in the whole world, of all the mighty empires that would ever rise, the God who created everything, chose to take up residence with this one band of escaped slaves. From that moment on, if a foreigner wanted a relationship with the one true God, he had to go through this family. They were God's firstborn son.

As you read through the story of Exodus, you must bear that in mind, this is a story about God rescuing an unlikely group of people, a family of slaves. Consider how that truth is played out in these three instances:

1. When the Israelites celebrate and worship, after crossing the Red Sea, you have to see the significance of that moment. The God of heaven just brought the world's mightiest and most oppressive nation to its knees, crippling them militarily and economically on behalf of a group of slaves.

2. When God gives the Israelites instructions for the tabernacle, he isn't just trying to give them a list of complicated rules to see if they'll obey them. He is crowing them with honor and beauty by filling craftsmen with the Holy Spirit and having them create a beautiful and intricate tent, so God can live with his people.

3. When the Israelites worship the calf, they are breaking God's heart. He has given them such a marvelous gift and they have shown disdain for his gift, for God Himself. But even after that, God still filled the tent with his glory at the very end of the book.

I Am Not One of these People

Ok, so here is where it gets personal. I have to realize this book isn't about me. I am a white, middle-class, American. I have no personal experience with oppression or slavery. Even in my collective memory, my people have never been oppressed as slaves.

Of course, to be honest, my people have been the oppressors. My people have been the slave-holders. My people built their nation on the backs of slaves. That's true of my nation and it has been true of many nations: The United Kingdom, Rome, Greece, Babylon, etc.

So, I have to recognize I am going to naturally have a difficult time, sitting on a padded church pew with a suit and tie, identifying with a story of how slaves felt after 400 years of oppression. But I don't know that I'm supposed to identify with the Jews.

I am a Gentile

I'm a Gentile and I am supposed to identify with the Gentiles. I have to put myself in the story as an Egyptian or a Canaanite. I have to ask myself, if I lived at this time, would I would have said, "This group of slaves is favored by God. Even though their road looks like it might be filled with struggle and sorrow, I think I would be better off hitching my wagon to theirs"?

I have to break allegiance with my gods, the idols of my people, and swear allegiance to the God of Abraham, Isaac, and Jacob. I have to be one of the Egyptians who left the mighty empire of Egypt and went along with this group of slaves. If someone like me were to picture themselves as part of the Exodus story, that's probably how we should do so, as an Egyptian who joined the escaped slaves.

EXODUS

Jesus, God's True Son

This is why the Exodus is a beautiful picture of the Gospel. When Jesus showed up on the Earth, Rome was the new Egypt. But sadly, some of the Jews had become like Gentiles. They manipulated and oppressed their fellow man. They were filled with hatred, bitterness, and violence. They were not loyal, in their hearts, to the God of Israel.

So Jesus became the new Israel. The true Israel. God's true firstborn Son. He offered to lead anyone, Jew or Gentile, out of bondage and into freedom if they would follow him. And he is still making that offer. The only way to the Father is through him.

But in order to be rescued by him and become God's people, we have to break allegiance with the gods of our nation. We have to join ourselves to a lowly and oppressed man, who died a shameful death. We have to be willing to follow him even to our own shameful deaths, knowing that on the other side – when he returns – we will be crowned with glory and honor.

The only way to the Father is through Israel's Messiah. Are we willing to forsake our idols and clothe ourselves in His shame and lowliness? If we are, we get to become children of God, heirs of the promises God made to Abraham. We get to become living stones in the glorious, beautiful, and intricate temple of God.

Summary

That's it, if you want to become God's child, you have to humble yourself and give your allegiance to the God of Israel. That's the story of Exodus and that's the Gospel story.

LEVITICUS

The book of Leviticus is a strange book, especially to our ears. There is a lot of talk about blood, fat, and entrails. Most Christians speed-read through Leviticus and say, when they are finished, "I'm so glad we don't live under Old Testament law anymore." When I read Leviticus in one sitting, I thought to myself, "I wish people would stop saying that." That's really not how we should feel when we read this book.

God is Holy

I think most of us have the wrong idea about the word "holy." We tend to think it means "morally good." We assume when someone says, "God is holy," it means God is really, really good. God certainly is good, but that's not what "holy" means.

When we say, "God is holy" it means, "God is otherly." It means he is totally, completely, and fundamentally different than anyone or anything else. He is one-of-a-kind. He is himself and no other is like him.

God Desires Closeness

It may be hard for us to see the big picture, through all the blood and guts, but this book is about God wanting to dwell with His chosen people, Israel. He wants to be in close proximity to them. He wants to live right there in their camp. Isn't that beautiful and amazing? The God of heaven wants to live in a tent, so he can be close to His people.

There is, however, one problem with God dwelling with his people. The problem is that God is holy and people are…well…people. When people, in their unclean state, come into the presence of a holy God, they die. In love, God put a separation between Himself and people so they don't immediately die.

But don't think "unclean" means sinful. Many of the things that made a person "unclean" had nothing to do with personal sin. Things like disease, death, and blood were simply symbols of the fact that Israel (like all humanity) was still an exiled people. These things were symbolic reminders of their humanity and their mortality.

For instance, we shouldn't read the laws about leprosy or bodily emissions as allegories about personal sin. We should read these laws and understand that ordinary human beings are all exiled from the tree of life. That's why we live in a world of disease, blood, and death.

When ordinary daily living brought Israelites into contact with these symbols of their mortality, then they became ceremonially unclean and separated from their holy God.

But God loves his people too much to allow humanity to remain estranged from him. He put the Levitical system in place to make Israel incrementally clean, so He could dwell in their presence.

Pointing Forward to Jesus

There is so much more I could say about Leviticus, but I will close simply by rejoicing in the fact that the whole book points forward to Jesus. He is our perfect High Priest, who has come to make us permanently clean by offering himself, once and for all. As a result, through Jesus, God can take up his residence with us and in us.

God has always wanted to live with his people in harmony. The Levitical system was a temporary measure, but Jesus came to offer himself in love as the permanent solution.

NUMBERS

We call it "Numbers," but the Jews call it, "In the Wilderness." I much prefer their title. The title "Numbers," makes it sound like the book is just about the censuses that were taken; it is so much more than that.

God's Wrath

One of the major themes of this book seems to be the wrath of God. Israel makes God angry over and over and over again. They are punished (severely) several times throughout the book. Thousands of Israelites die because of their sins.

But one thing I noticed was the distinction God made between unintentional and intentional sins. Even in the midst of his anger and wrath, God was providing ways for his people to find forgiveness when they unintentionally strayed. But he also "cut off" from his people those who did not trust him and "high handedly" rebelled against him.

God understands and sympathizes with human weakness and frailty, but he will not tolerate open rebellion in the midst of his camp.

God's Covenant Faithfulness

Even though Israel proved to be a stubborn and rebellious people, God did not abandon them during their 40 years of wilderness wandering. He did not destroy them and start over (even when He wanted to do just that).

He stuck with Israel. He made a promise to them and he would keep his promise no matter the cost.

This becomes a central theme to the entire Bible. In fact, the book of Romans highlights this theme. In spite of people's unfaithfulness, God is always faithful to the promises he makes. He always does what he says he will do.

The Promised Land

As we noted in the chapter on Genesis, the land (or the earth) is a prominent character in the Bible. Unfortunately, we have a tendency to assume God is all about non-material things and it is only silly humans who care about material things, like pieces of property.

The truth is, the God of the Bible is also very concerned about material things. God wants to give the land to his people as a perpetual inheritance. He wants his people to experience the fruitful blessings of the land. He wants the land to be undefiled with violence. And above all, he wants to dwell in the land with his people.

The Bible is a very "earthy" book. The theme is never, "Don't be concerned about material things because material things are just an illusion." That is Buddhism or Greek philosophy, but not Christianity. In the Bible, and particularly now the book of Numbers, the theme is: "The earth shall be filled with the glory of the Lord."

God Has Not Changed

During their wandering, the people were cursed because of their disbelief and rebellion. But in his mercy, God instructed Moses to lift up a bronze serpent so that anyone who looked upon it would be healed. Jesus ties the book of Numbers to himself, saying, "Just as Moses lifted up the snake in the desert, in the same way the son of man must be lifted up, so that everyone who believes in him may share in the life of God's new age" (John 3:14-15, *The Kingdom New Testament*).

Look upon Jesus in obedient faith and you will receive a life for the age to come. That is the promise of the Gospel. The same God who lifted the curse in the wilderness and brought His people into the Promised Land is lifting our curse and will bring to us our inheritance.

God wiped away the old world and gave Noah a new world through the flood. God wiped away the old land of Canaan and gave Israel a new land through the conquest. He will also wipe away the old world of sin and death and give us "a new heavens and a new earth in which righteousness dwells" (2 Peter 3:13). Our inheritance is being stored up for us and the God who does not change will deliver on all of his promises.

DEUTERONOMY

Reading whole books in one sitting can be incredibly intimidating at first, but if you make it through the Torah (Genesis-Deuteronomy) you will be doing very well and will probably be beginning to discover what I discovered, it is not nearly as difficult as I thought it would be and it is far more rewarding than I expected. Our title for Deuteronomy comes from two Greek words, "deuteros" and "nomos" which mean "second" and "law." In other words, this book is about the second giving of the Law to the people of Israel. Though "Law" – or the "Torah" – might better be understood as "instruction."

The people of Israel had wandered in the wilderness and now it was finally time to take possession of Canaan, which God had promised to their forefathers. But before they took possession, Moses reminded them of where they came from and how they were supposed to live as God's delivered and sanctified people.

God's Grace

If you gloss over the book of Deuteronomy, or take a few passages out of context, you might think this is a book about works, "Do this and good things will happen, do that and bad things will happen." But reading it that way really misses the big picture.

Moses reminds Israel over and over, they don't deserve to receive the land. They are receiving it as a gift because of God's love for them and the promises he made to their forefathers. God is keeping the promises of his covenant with them, in spite of the fact that Israel has been stubborn and rebellious for the last forty years.

The Purpose of Obedience

Again, if we're not careful we will read this story as saying the Promised Land would be their wages for obedience to the Law. But again, that misses the point.

From the very beginning, Moses tells Israel that the purpose of their obedience was so that they might be a light to other nations. God wanted the Gentile nations to see Israel and say to themselves, "Surely this great nation is a wise and understanding people." Israel's obedience to the Torah of God was supposed to point the nations to the God of the Torah. As a kingdom, Israel was supposed to act as a priesthood to the other nations. They were supposed to reflect the glory of God into the world and be a blessing to the nations on behalf of God; so that the whole world might know the one true God.

Care for the Vulnerable

One of the primary aspects of the Law on which Deuteronomy focuses is caring for three special groups of people: the fatherless, widow, and immigrant. It was the job of every Israelite to provide for these people.

In other civilizations, these groups might have been seen as a drag on the society. After all, they contribute little and cost much. But amongst God's people, the fatherless, widow, and immigrant were to enjoy a favored status. They were to be cared for by the whole community.

Return from Exile

The land of Canaan is described as being a paradise. A place like the Garden of Eden. In fact, it's almost as if Israel taking possession of the Promised Land is like the first group of humans returning from exile to the Garden. But sadly, throughout the book, Israel's own fall and their own coming exile are already imminent. Like Adam and Eve, like all humanity, Israel would inevitably fall and be exiled from God's paradise.

Their coming fall, however, would not stop God from fulfilling his promises. Someday in the distant future, after their fall and exile, they would be given the opportunity to repent of their sins, be forgiven, and dwell once again in the land. But this would only be possible through divine intervention; God would have to be the one to circumcise their hearts.

Only after this great act of God, would they be able to fulfill the greatest commands of the Torah: loving God with all their heart, soul, and strength and loving their neighbor as themselves.

The Good News of Jesus

In keeping with that promise, this is the Good News that was announced to the gathered people of Israel on the Day of Pentecost, "Repent and be baptized every one of you in the name of Jesus Christ for the forgiveness of your sins, and you will receive the gift of the Holy Spirit" (Acts 2:38).

Through Jesus, Israel and the nations are all being delivered from exile. Sins are being forgiven. Our hearts are being changed so that we truly begin to love him and love others. Someday soon our deliverance will be complete; sin and death will be no more and we will "eat of the tree of life, which is in the paradise of God" (Revelation 2:7).

Until then, let us be what Jesus was and what Israel was called to be, a royal priesthood whose faithfulness points the nations to our God.

JOSHUA

Many people struggle to understand the story of Joshua and the conquest of Canaan. They understandably wonder, "Is Jesus of Nazareth, who told His followers to love their enemies and turn the other cheek, really the exact representation of the God who ordered warfare in the book of Joshua?"

In Light of the Torah

The book of Joshua, like all books of the Bible, must be read in light of the Torah. It is impossible to understand what is going on in the story of the Conquest unless you put it in the context of the backstory of Genesis-Deuteronomy.

As we have noted in previous chapters, the earth is a major character in the Bible. The Canaanites had polluted and defiled the land through idolatry and violence. The book of Leviticus says the land was vomiting out the Canaanites. The voice of a multitude's blood was crying out to the Lord from the ground. God's good creation was groaning for deliverance.

The conquest should be seen in the same light as the Flood. The wickedness of the Canaanites had reached epic proportions; the land had to be wiped clean. But this time, when God wiped the land clean, he would take up residence in the land. He would make it "holy ground" and populate the land with a holy people – a kingdom of priests – and they would be tasked with blessing all the nations of the world.

JOSHUA

Canaanites Had Been Warned

From the very beginning of the book, it is obvious the Lord's reputation preceded him. The Canaanites knew the power of the Lord and knew they had been condemned by him. They were terrified. Some even threw themselves on God's mercy.

God didn't just suddenly surprise the Canaanite people with swift and terrible justice. For over four hundred years, God delayed punishing the Canaanites. For forty years, His people marched around the land in the wilderness; giving the Canaanites more time to repent. And for seven days, Israel marched around the walls of Jericho. Proving that the Lord is patient toward people, "not wishing that any should perish, but that all should reach repentance" (2 Peter 3:9).

When the Day of the Lord finally came, it came like a thief in the night and the world of the Canaanites was destroyed by fire and sword.

Put to the Sword vs. Drive Out

There are a few verses in Joshua that, if taken all by themselves, make the reader believe the idea of the conquest was to kill every man, woman, and child in the land. This is why reading whole books, rather than taking passages out of context, is so important. There is certainly a lot of warfare in this book, but the phrase "drive out" is repeated even more than any language about killing.

Taken as a whole, it sounds like many of the Canaanites recognized the impending judgment of God and fled from their cities. The ones who died were the hard-hearted ones who decided to fight against God. The fact that they were "driven out" of the land should remind us of Adam and Eve (and later, Cain) who were themselves "driven out" by God. The Canaanites, like Adam and Eve, were being driven out of paradise.

Every Canaanite man, woman, and child was cursed and condemned by their sin. As God said to Adam and Eve, the Canaanites were essentially being told, "You will surely die." Either they would die in warfare or in exile.

The Lord is the Warrior of His People

Many people think the book of Joshua proves that God is somehow "pro-war." But when taken as a whole, the first six books of the Bible make it very clear that the thing God most hates is people shedding one another's blood. After the conquest of Canaan, Israel was to have the world's most unusual defense system and war policy.

Israel was not supposed to accumulate weapons of war either for offensive or defensive campaigns. In fact, even during the conquest, when they captured chariots, they were supposed to destroy them and hamstring the horses. Isn't that bizarre? God's people were not allowed to own the best military equipment of the day. They were told over and over again not to put any confidence in military strength. God was the warrior of Israel. It was not Israel's sword or bow which conquered the land, it was their God.

God wanted to continue to be their protector and their peace. As such, he would not tolerate them accumulating or putting their trust in weapons of war. That was part of the idolatry the Gentile nations practiced. Sadly, it would be the sort of idolatry Israel would soon practice as well.

Pointing to Jesus

When Jesus came into the world, the wickedness of the world had once again reached epic proportions. The earth was groaning for deliverance and the people deserved to be judged and driven out. Jerusalem itself had become a crossroads of both Jewish and Gentile rebellion.

But instead of driving the rebellious out of the land, Jesus became accursed in the people's place. He let the consequences of the world's rebellion fall on him. The only way to bring the exiles back into fellowship with God was to take on the form of an exile.

In so doing, Jesus is expelling evil from the land by forgiving sins, so that God can move into the earth by first moving into the hearts of his people. The earth is now being populated with a kingdom of priests; meek and gentle peace-makers. And one day, he will return to finish what he started.

JUDGES

When I was a kid, I loved the book of Judges. It was full of violence and gore. There were tent pegs, strong men, lions, death, and destruction. I loved it. It made me think God would be an awesome movie director. Unfortunately, I was reading the book of Judges all wrong. The book of Judges is a collection of some of the worst stories in the Bible. And if you don't recognize them as the worst stories in the Bible, you're probably not reading them correctly.

Stories That Make You Weep

Israel was supposed to drive the Canaanites out of the land of Israel; but unfortunately, Israel not only failed to drive the Canaanites out, they became exactly like the Canaanites in the worst possible ways. They raped, murdered, worshiped idols, and even sacrificed their own children. They were overcome by pride, lust, vengeance, cowardice, and idolatry.

Even the good guys, the judges whom God sent to lead and deliver His people, were often as wicked as the people they were supposed to lead. From the beginning to the end, the judges themselves seem to get progressively worse.

One judge sacrificed his young daughter. One judge married a Philistine, slept with a prostitute, and shacked up with a woman who tried to have him killed on multiple occasions. One judge said he didn't want to be the people's king, but named his son, "Abimelech" (My-Father-Is-King). That warped young man, by the way, grew up and murdered all of his brothers so he could rule.

The book of Judges is absolutely spilling over with blood. People were whipped, stabbed, crushed, and burned with fire. Sadly, our glorification of violence and bloodshed makes young boys read this book and say, "Cool," when we all ought to have tears streaming down our cheeks when we read these stories. There is nothing "cool" about it.

Lose-Lose Situations

On at least two occasions in Judges, ridiculous vows were made. Jephthah swore he would offer as a burnt offering whatever came out from the doors of his house to meet him when he returned home. As you probably know, his daughter came out the door. Jephthah was in a moral dilemma.

God had specifically told His people, "There shall not be found among you anyone who burns his son or his daughter as an offering" (Deuteronomy 18:10). But God had also told them, "If a man vows a vow to the Lord, or swears an oath to bind himself by a pledge, he shall not break his word. He shall do according to all that proceeds out of his mouth" (Numbers 30:2).

Jephthah was in a lose-lose situation. Which law should he violate? Should he sacrifice his daughter or break his vow? Which law was more important? As you probably know, Jephthah chose to sacrifice his daughter.

Near the end of the book, this same theme and dilemma is brought up again. The men of Israel chose to murder men, women, and children, as well as kidnap a bunch of young women, rather than break a vow they made to the Lord.

Was that the right choice? Is YHWH really like pagan gods? Would He really want someone to murder rather than break their vow? Of course not!

Judges in Hebrews 11

Gideon, Barak, Samson, and Jephthah are mentioned briefly in Hebrews 11. Many assume this means, in spite of their glaring faults, these men were actually pretty pious men after all.

But the book of Judges says that Gideon beat and killed his brethren out of vengeance and ended his life in idolatry. Barak was a coward. Samson was a womanizer who died taking personal vengeance on his enemies. Jephthah sacrificed his own daughter because of his warped theology.

The Hebrew writer is not saying these men were good men. He is not saying they were religious men. He is not saying we ought to imitate them. He is trying to inspire faith by reminding his audience that these men (at least at one point in their lives) trusted God to do amazing things through them.

These men "escaped the edge of the sword, were made strong out of weakness, became mighty in war, put foreign armies to flight" (Hebrews 11:34), but it was God who gets the credit. The emphasis is NOT on the moral uprightness of these people but on the power of God. They had "faith" in the sense that they trusted in God's power to help them in seemingly hopeless, seemingly impossible, situations.

Their Sin is the Point

It seems so hard for us to realize there is really no one to imitate in the biblical stories of Judges. The point isn't to find little nuggets of what they did well and make those moral imperatives. The proper response to the book of Judges is lament.

We should weep that Israel followed the way of all mankind, doing "what was right in their own eyes." They had no one of strong moral character to lead them. They had no one to show them that God desires mercy and not sacrifice. They had no one to plead the cause of the widow, the sojourner, and the fatherless. They had a few shepherds, but they did not have a "good shepherd."

Even when – through the power of God's Spirit – the judges were strong in one area, they were weak in other areas. All we know about some judges is that they judged and they died. When they were overcome by death, Israel reverted to her old ways and that judge's long legacy came to nothing. It was like he had never lived, because there was no long-lasting change.

The book of Judges leaves us longing for a selfless judge, a righteous judge, a judge who will both defeat our enemies and help the helpless, and a judge who will not be overcome by death. In Jesus, we have received such a Judge. He is the one to whom every judge's strength points, and the one who is not beset with any of their weaknesses.

SAMUEL

When someone became king in Israel, a priest would pour oil on that man's head and he would then be known as the Lord's "anointed." The Hebrew word for "anointed" is "messiah." The books of Samuel form the story of two messiahs, Saul and David.

Notice the Contrasts

In order to understand the message of Samuel, it seems to me, you must constantly be looking for the contrasts throughout the story. In fact, the second verse of the book mentions a contrast, "Peninnah had children, but Hannah had no children."

The next major contrast is between Eli and Samuel. Because Eli's sons are horribly wicked and Eli does not restrain them, the Lord tells him, "I will raise up for myself a faithful priest, who shall do according to what is in my heart and in my mind. And I will build him a sure house, and he shall go in and out before my anointed forever."

But the primary contrast is between David and Saul. When we first meet both men, they are taking care of their fathers' animals. However, Saul has lost his father's donkeys and cannot find them, while David fends off a lion and a bear to protects his father's flock. Saul is a coward who hides in the luggage, but David is a warrior who fights giants. In fact, a song of contrast is mentioned several times, "Saul has struck down his thousands, and David his ten thousands."

Notice the Comparisons

There are also several subtle, and not so subtle, comparisons throughout the story. One of the obvious comparisons is that Israel wants to be just like the other nations. The thing that is supposed to set Israel apart is that the Lord is her warrior King. He fights Israel's battles for them, but the people of Israel say they want to "be like all the nations, and that our king may judge us and go out before us and fight our battles." Saul becomes another living example of corrupt human kings.

Saul is also compared to earlier judges of Israel. For example, Saul makes a rash vow, like Jephthah, promising to kill anyone who eats anything before he has had victory over his enemies. Unfortunately, Saul's son Jonathan ate some honey, so Saul swore to keep his promise and kill his son. Thankfully, the godly people of Israel redeemed Jonathan's life so he was not put to death.

Two Messiahs, Two Kingdoms

Throughout most of the first volume, there are two anointed kings in Israel. There is Saul, a man after the people's own heart. And there is David, a man after God's own heart. Or to put it another way, Saul's kingdom is an earthly reign, but David's kingdom is a heavenly kingdom. When David was at his best, we got just a small taste of what it might be like for the Lord God to truly reign through a "messiah."

These two kingdoms existed side-by-side for many years. David, the messiah after God's own heart, gathered to himself, "everyone who was in distress, and everyone who was in debt, and everyone who was bitter in soul." But Saul persecuted David unrelentingly.

Surprisingly, in submissive humility, David would not raise his hand against Saul, because Saul had also been anointed by the Lord to serve a purpose.

The Beginning of the End

Sadly, even David was not the perfect messiah. He was probably as close as any man ever came, but he gave into temptation. In the weakness of his flesh, he lusted, fornicated, murdered, enslaved, and trusted in the strength of chariots and armies. In the end, David turned out to be somewhat like other human kings; and in his lifetime we already see the cracks starting to form in Israel. We begin to see some of the things which will eventually lead to Israel's exile.

That said, David gave us a tiny glimpse of what it might be like for the Lord to reign over the earth through a man. His strength makes us say,

"Perhaps there is a human who could do the job," but his weakness makes us say, "No, the only one who can reign is the Lord." It turns out, of course, both of those sentiments are correct.

The Implications

To me, the implications of this story are incredibly important. We live in a time when there are two kingdoms. There is the kingdom of the earth (which has countless manifestations around the globe) and then there is the kingdom of heaven. Though the kingdom of earth has been anointed by God to carry out a task in the world (Romans 13:1-7), that ought not to be the kingdom to which God's people give their allegiance.

God has anointed his own Son to be the Messiah of the whole world. The Lord God is reigning through a divine human being, who is the first of a new creation. We are the people in distress and debt and bitter in soul, who have been gathered to the Lord's Anointed. Like David, and like Jesus, we humbly submit to earthly rulers and refuse to raise our hand against them in rebellion, but our true allegiance is to heaven's King because our citizenship is in the heavenly kingdom.

As we wait for the reign of human kingdoms to come to an end, we patiently endure and we sing the Psalms to the Lord, "Your kingdom is an everlasting kingdom, and your dominion endures throughout all generations" (Psalm 145:13).

KINGS

The story of 1 and 2 Kings is a tremendous and heartbreaking story. But most importantly, it is a story which we must know if we are going to understand what it means to be a part of the kingdom of God.

A Tragic Story

The book of Kings covers less than 400 years and it tells the story of how God's people disregarded his law and ended up in exile. It is much like the story of Adam and Eve. In the beginning, the people are living in paradise, but because of their disobedience, they are driven out to the east. This is why 1 and 2 Kings really need to be read together because the reader is supposed to see the difference between the beginning of the story and the end of the story.

For instance, in 1 Kings 3, there is the famous story of two women fighting over the custody of a child. There was a child who died and a child who was alive. Each woman claimed the living child as her own. Solomon wisely offered to cut the child in half, knowing the true mother would surrender custody rather than let her child be killed.

This story is contrasted with something that happens in 2 Kings 6, during a siege of Samaria. Like Solomon, the king is asked to settle a dispute between two women. In this story as well, there is a dead child and a living child. However, in this story, the woman who comes to the king is upset because she and another woman were so hungry they had decided to boil and eat their babies. But after they ate this woman's baby, the second mother hid her living child.

The book of Kings is filled with these types of contrasts so the reader can grasp the epic tragedy of Israel's fall. When Solomon reigned, "silver was as common in Jerusalem as stone." But by the end of the story, the king of Judah and most of God's people are prisoners and slaves in Babylon. Solomon built a beautiful and glorious temple. But by the end of the story, the temple is an ash heap. When Solomon reigned, foreign dignitaries came to marvel at Israel and her king. But by the end of the story, Israel has become "a byword among all peoples."

Solomon's Sin

For some reason, we often think of Solomon as one of the good kings of Israel. But in spite of the wisdom God gave him, Solomon brought idolatry to the kingdom. Solomon was the king who set Israel on a trajectory towards exile.

In fact, the author of Kings is somewhat subtle in introducing Solomon's sin. When we, as modern readers, read about Solomon's thousands of horses and chariots, and we read about all of his silver and gold, we are impressed. However, we should NOT be impressed. We should be horrified. We should be shouting at the pages of our Bibles, "No! No, Solomon! Don't do it! This is exactly what the Lord said not to do."

From the very beginning of his reign, Solomon was a worldly king. In Deuteronomy 17:16-17, God had given these instructions for future kings of Israel:

1. Don't acquire many horses.

2. Don't acquire many wives.

3. Don't acquire excessive silver and gold.

These three things were like kings' forbidden fruit. Solomon wasted no time before he picked the fruit and took a bite.

Horses and Chariots

One of the recurring themes in the book is horses and chariots. A chariot was like the tank of the ancient world. It was the most advanced military technology and the king with the most chariots was confident he would prevail in battle.

But Israel was supposed to be different. They weren't supposed to think like that. They weren't supposed to believe they were in danger from armies with chariots. They were supposed to believe God was their shield and defender. They were supposed to believe it didn't matter how many chariots the armies of men had because chariots were no match for God.

But from the beginning of the story, their trust was misplaced. They trusted in horses and chariots. They trusted in alliances with other nations. They trusted in "gods" of other nations.

God continually tried to open their eyes and help them see his unseen army and his chariots of fire; the hosts he leads are greater and more powerful than any nation on earth. He tried to help them realize he could defeat world empires without a shot being fired. He could cause kings of mighty armies to hear noises or rumors and retreat from the battle in fear.

God tried to get his people to walk by faith, but they were afraid and they put their trust in things they could see.

Resurrection and Restoration

The story of Kings points forward to Jesus in many wonderful ways. First, of course, in the anticipation of a Davidic king, one like Josiah, who would end the exile and bring the kingdom of heaven. But the prophets of God also point forward to Jesus and his ministry.

Both Elijah and Elisha bring dead people back to life. In fact, the occurrences in this book might be the first times in the Bible when people are brought back to life. As people whose primary hope is tied up in the coming resurrection, these accounts should be of great significance to us.

Consider the Shunammite woman in 2 Kings. She trusted the Lord and her son was raised to life. But also, after her sojourn, "The king appointed an official for her, saying, 'Restore all that was hers, together with all the produce of the fields from the day that she left the land until now.'" She trusted in the Lord and her family experienced resurrection and they inherited the earth.

But my favorite story is that of the man who was buried in Elisha's tomb. As soon as his dead body touched Elisha's bones, he was raised to life. What a tremendous foreshadowing of the Gospel. All of us who are buried with Jesus will be brought to life by him.

When Will We Learn?

When are God's people today going to learn from the story of which we are a part? When are we going to learn to stop trusting in gold and chariots and alliances with worldly nations? When are we going to realize the Messiah has come and ended our exile? When are we going to realize he raises the dead and we do not have to fear those who can destroy the body?

ISAIAH

As I read Isaiah this time around, it occurred to me that to understand Jesus, a person really needs to read Isaiah. Sadly, many of us do not understand our own Lord because we do not see him in light of Isaiah's prophecies. Oh, we know, "He was pierced for our transgressions; he was crushed for our iniquities," but we don't know the context. We don't see the big picture Isaiah was painting about the end of exile and the beginning of the new creation.

Isaiah's Context

Because we are following the TaNaK order of Scripture, we went straight from Kings to Isaiah. That is helpful because it helps us understand the context in which Isaiah is prophesying. Isaiah's ministry lasted from King Uzziah to King Hezekiah; or in other words, 2 Kings chapters 15 through 20.

Isaiah prophesied when the Northern Kingdom of Israel was destroyed and carried off into exile by Assyria. And, during Isaiah's day, the Southern Kingdom of Judah looked as if it would be destroyed by hoards of Assyrians as well. But Isaiah told Judah to trust in the Lord and not in military alliances with other nations. He also warned them that they would eventually be carried off into exile by Babylon because of their own sins. So the idea of being exiled or driven out "to the east" is a major theme in the book of Isaiah.

ISAIAH

In the chapter on Deuteronomy, we said Canaan was supposed to remind us of the Garden of Eden. The Promised Land of Israel was a paradise where God and men lived together. But just like humanity was driven out "to the east" (Genesis 3:24), Israel and Judah were also driven out to the east and scattered amongst the nations.

God as a Redeemer

Throughout the book of Isaiah, we see the words ransom, redeem, and redemption. To understand those ideas, you have to think back to the books of Moses (Genesis-Deuteronomy). You have to think about how God "redeemed" the people out of Egyptian bondage, "I am the Lord, and I will bring you out from under the burdens of the Egyptians, and I will deliver you from slavery to them, and I will redeem you with an outstretched arm and with great acts of judgment" (Exodus 6:6).

When we think of being "redeemed," we often think of a business transaction. One person purchases something from someone else. But that's not always the biblical idea of redemption. When God redeems His people, He doesn't pay anyone for them. The whole cosmos belongs to Him, who would He pay? When God redeems His people, it is about bringing them back from exile and giving them the land.

This is an incredibly important theme in Isaiah. This book helps us to realize, God's plan is not just to redeem Israel, but to redeem people from all nations. God will build a road that will lead people from exile back to Zion. Isaiah says the Lord will make the wilderness of Zion "like Eden" and her desert like the "garden of the Lord."

In fact, the Lord will recreate the whole heavens and the earth for His redeemed people. The Lord says, "The wolf and the lamb shall graze together; the lion shall eat straw like the ox, and dust shall be the serpent's food. They shall not hurt or destroy in all my holy mountain."

God as a Judge

Isaiah has plenty of beautiful promises, but also plenty of judgment. He makes it very clear, the Lord is God of the whole earth and he will judge every nation. The oppressed will be set free and the oppressors will be judged. There is no injustice that will go unpunished.

But there also seems to be the idea that, because Israel belongs to the Lord, they would take the lion's share of humanity's punishment. It's like when an individual sins, he contributes a drop of filth to a huge cup. As each person in the world sins, more drops are added to the cup until it reaches the point when it is full and must be poured out as punishment or someone must drink it.

Israel would be the one to drink the cup down to its dregs. But how would they survive? They would survive because someone would stand in for them and drink the cup in their place. Through this plan, God would swallow up the veil that was spread over all nations; he would swallow up death forever. God was executing a plan to bring humanity back from exile and give them a whole new world without death.

But God knew then, just as He knows now, not everyone will submit to His plan. He reaches out His arms, but not everyone wants to be saved. Many will reject His offer to redeem. The book of Isaiah ends with these words:

> *For as the new heavens and the new earth that I make shall remain before me, says the Lord, so shall your offspring and your name remain. From new moon to new moon, and from Sabbath to Sabbath, all flesh shall come to worship before me, declares the Lord. And they shall go out and look on the dead bodies of the men who have rebelled against me. For their worm shall not die, their fire shall not be quenched, and they shall be an abhorrence to all flesh.*

Understanding Jesus

So if we are going to understand Jesus, we have to understand the hope and expectation Isaiah lays out for us. If we read the Gospel accounts first and assume we know and understand Jesus, then we read Isaiah through that lens, we may misunderstand both Jesus and Isaiah. But if we start with Isaiah, letting the hope and anticipation properly build, then we will understand why Jesus' coming is truly Good News for the world.

JEREMIAH

Jeremiah prophesied, and later witnessed, the destruction of Jerusalem. He had the unpleasant task of warning the people of Jerusalem that their enemies were going to win. His neighbors hated him for his message of doom and gloom. In fact, they very much wanted to put him to death for his lack of patriotism. Just imagine, if your country was in the midst of war, how much would you appreciate your neighbor predicting that your country was going to lose? That was Jeremiah's lot in life, to speak against his own people because of their sin.

Ruin and Waste

The major theme of Jeremiah's prophecies was judgment. Primarily, judgment against Jerusalem, but also judgment against all the wicked nations of the earth.

There is a common picture we see in this book, the idea that when a city has been judged, it will lie forever in "ruin and waste." That's a powerful image. God wants people to know that their cities stand strong, beautiful, and organized, but when he brings judgment upon them, wild animals would be the only things that live there. And he wants them to know, even though their cities seem to stand as monuments to their greatness, eventually, they will lie in ruins as a monument to God's sovereignty.

Jerusalem, of course, would suffer that fate. The glory of Jerusalem would come undone and the citizens would end up once again as slaves. Israel's story had been reversed. They had been freed from slavery and come into the Promised Land, but now they were slaves again. Everything had fallen apart. Everything had come undone.

Jeremiah Speaks of "Hell"

It's interesting that Jesus uses language and images from Jeremiah to warn the people of his day. Jeremiah spoke of a certain valley, "the valley of the son of Hinnom." In that cursed valley, people had sacrificed their infant sons and daughters to the idol, Molech.

Through Jeremiah, God warned them that their wickedness would be judged in that very same valley:

> *This place shall no more be called Topheth, or the Valley of the Son of Hinnom, but the Valley of Slaughter. And in this place I will make void the plans of Judah and Jerusalem, and will cause their people to fall by the sword before their enemies, and by the hand of those who seek their life. I will give their dead bodies for food to the birds of the air and to the beasts of the earth.*

When Jesus talked about people being thrown into "hell," he was using the word, "Gehenna," which is a reference to this valley. Jesus was warning his people, like Jeremiah, if they continued to reject the word of the Lord, this would be their fate.

Living as Exiles

After Nebuchadnezzar carried off the first wave of exiles, there were still false prophets trying to reassure the people the exile would only last two years. Jeremiah had to send a letter to the people to tell them the exile would be seventy years and most of them would die as slaves in Babylon. What a horrible letter to have to send to your people.

But in that letter, we read how God expected his people to live while they were exiles. Even though they were citizens of Jerusalem, they were supposed to build houses, plant gardens, get married, have babies, and seek the welfare of the city of Babylon. They were supposed to be faithful to their God and a blessing to their captors.

When Peter sent his first epistle, he used this same language to help Christians understand how they are supposed to live in the world. He wrote in 1 Peter 2:11-12:

> *Beloved, I urge you as sojourners and exiles to abstain from the passions of the flesh, which wage war against your soul. Keep your conduct among the Gentiles honorable, so that when they speak against you as evildoers, they may see your good deeds and glorify God on the day of visitation.*

Christians, living dispersed in the world, are supposed to be faithful to God and a blessing to the nations we inhabit. And just like the exiles in Babylon, we wait with anticipation.

Future Blessings

Though most of Jeremiah is doom and gloom, we do get a few glimpses of hope. The Lord says his commitment to Israel is unbreakable. He says it would be easier to break the fixed order of the sun, moon, stars, and roaring waves of the sea than to break his commitment to Israel.

He says, no matter what happens, "the offspring of Israel [will not] cease from being a nation before me forever." He promises he will restore them to the land and fix their hearts so they will be obedient to him forever, with his law written on their hearts.

Of course, you can see how these promises confused many people in the first century who heard the Gospel. They asked Paul questions like, "Why are you preaching that Israel is cut off? That can't happen! Why are you preaching that the Gentiles are heirs of the promises God made to us?"

Paul's answer was shocking. His answer was that God hadn't rejected Israel at all, but God was remaking Israel. The new Israel was everyone – both Jew and Gentile – who had faith in Jesus. Paul preached that when a person was baptized into Jesus, he became a descendant of Abraham and an heir of the world (see Galatians 3; Romans 4).

This is what the Gospel is all about: Jesus' followers are Israel and are the ones who will inherit everything God promised to Abraham's descendants because we are Abraham's descendants by faith. In the meantime, we are to live as exiles, faithful to our God and a blessing to the nations, while we wait for "the day of visitation."

EZEKIEL

The book of Ezekiel is not as hard to read in a day as you might suppose. It is a bit long and there are a few apocalyptic visions, filled with pretty bizarre symbolic images, but most of the book is pretty straightforward. As you read, you will probably notice that Jesus borrowed a lot of parables and metaphors from Ezekiel and the book of Revelation also borrowed a lot of language from Ezekiel. Ezekiel is a book of judgment and hope. It describes God's plan to purge the evil from Israel and make them into a holy people forever.

Ezekiel, the Exile

Ezekiel was an exile in Babylon before the temple was destroyed in Jerusalem. He saw multiple visions, indicating that God's glory had left the temple and the temple would be destroyed. There were all kinds of people during this time preaching false visions, saying they had received a message from the Lord, but it was really just their own imaginations.

Can you imagine if an enemy nation invaded your country, chained you up, and shipped you far away? Can you imagine how desperate you would be for a message of hope? If someone told you, "This will all be over soon," and someone else told you, "More death and destruction are coming because God is very angry with us," to whom would you listen?

God told Ezekiel to sound the trumpet and give his people warning that more punishment, terrible punishment, was coming. God told Ezekiel the people wouldn't listen to his preaching; regardless, he should preach anyway.

How Sick Is Your Heart?

I will warn you, much of the book of Ezekiel isn't appropriate for children. Yep, that's right, there are books of the Bible that are PG-13 or greater. This is one of those books.

God describes his relationship with Israel with several different metaphors and parables. One of the most poignant stories describes Israel as a baby girl, all alone in a field. She is still covered in afterbirth because she had been cast out on the day of her birth. God found her and rescued her. She grew into a young woman and God married her and clothed her royally. But she "played the whore." Throughout the book, God describes Israel and Judah's idolatrous "whoring." They worshiped idols and sacrificed the blessings God had given them to other gods.

But it wasn't just idolatry in a traditional sense that was condemned as "whoring. It was also Israel's lustful desire to be protected by other nations that God called "playing the whore." When God's people made military alliances with Egypt or Assyria, to be protected by them, they were showing God that they really didn't trust in his divine protection. They lusted after horses, chariots, and soldiers. God was disgusted by their lust for military strength. He told them, "Because you did not hate bloodshed, therefore blood shall pursue you."

Lust for military strength brings military strength down upon you. But the one who trusts in the Lord with all of his heart, and loves the Lord with all of his heart, will be delivered. That was one of the most important lessons Israel needed to learn.

A New Heart

In spite of the harsh judgment God was pouring out on his people, he also promised he would one day gather them up from the nations to which they were dispersed. Like sheep that were scattered all over the hills, God would gather his people and be their shepherd. God promised to give them a new David to be their king, make an everlasting covenant with them, and bless them forever.

> *I will take you from the nations and gather you from all the countries and bring you into your own land. I will sprinkle clean water on you, and you shall be clean from all your uncleannesses, and from all your idols I will cleanse you. And I will give you a new heart, and a new spirit I will put within you. And I will remove the heart of stone from your flesh and give you a heart of flesh. And I will put my Spirit within you, and cause you to walk in my statutes and be careful to obey my rules.*

God was not only going to fix their situation, he was going to fix the people. He was going to cleanse them from their sin and give them a new heart and put his own Spirit within them, so they would be an obedient people. Not obedient in an outward and ritualistic way, but obedient from the heart. They would do the right sorts of things, not because the law told them to, but because they love the Lord their God with all of their heart, soul, and strength.

Resurrection and Restoration

When we say Jesus is "the Messiah," we are saying we believe he is the one who has fulfilled, is fulfilling, and will fulfill the visions of Ezekiel and the other prophets. We are saying Jesus has gathered up the lost sheep of Israel and also the Gentiles, who were sheep of another fold, and that he is shepherding us now and forever. We are also saying that Israel – and all humanity – were as dead as a valley of dry bones, but Jesus resurrected us and gave us God's Spirit and a new heart.

But it's more than that. Jesus has fulfilled and is fulfilling the visions of Ezekiel, but there is still a future hope. There is a future resurrection; a literal resurrection. And Ezekiel spoke about God's people inheriting the land forever. God will destroy every city of wickedness and everything will be desolate and waste, but then his people will say, "This land that was desolate has become like the garden of Eden."

The apostle Paul wrote that the followers of Jesus, both Jew and Gentile, are heirs of these promises. As he said to the church in Rome, "Abraham and his descendants received the promise that they would get the whole world" (ERV). All of creation and the children of God wait to be set free from our bondage to corruption (Romans 8:21). We wait for God's glory to be revealed and to receive our inheritance.

Because of sin, everything will become desolate and waste, but then it will "become like the garden of Eden," and we will be with our Lord forever. That is our hope.

MINOR PROPHETS

These twelve books, which we typically call "The Minor Prophets," were written by different authors to different audiences and span about 400 years of time. Even so, I found it incredibly enlightening to read through all twelve in one day. After all, at one time, these twelve books were actually all part of a single scroll, "The Book of the Twelve." And when you read them together, they tell a story that leaves you asking the question, "When will God keep his promises?"

The Arrangement of the Minor Prophets

The first set of six books are the books that came from the period of Assyrian power. About 700 years before the birth of Jesus, the Assyrian Empire destroyed the Northern Kingdom of Israel and took captives away into exile. These are the books of:

Hosea

Joel

Amos

Obadiah

MINOR PROPHETS

Jonah

Micah

The second set of books spans the time period of Assyria's decline and Babylon's rise to power. The Empire of Babylon destroyed the Southern Kingdom of Judah and took captives to Babylon. The temple in Jerusalem was destroyed, after a long siege, in the year 586 B.C. These are the books of:

Nahum

Habakkuk

Zephaniah

And finally, the third set of books were written after the Empire of Babylon fell to the Medo-Persian Empire and a trickle of Jews began to return to Jerusalem to start to rebuild their home. These are the books of:

Haggai

Zechariah

Malachi

The Wages of Sin is Death

These twelve books tell us that God is the sovereign judge, he takes sin seriously, and the people of every nation are brought before his throne to answer for their crimes. But what are the sorts of things God condemns? What makes God angry?

The answer to that question is what has really struck me hard during this particular journey through the Bible. Growing up, I thought God felt the same way about religious ceremonial laws as he did moral laws. I thought God was as likely to punish someone for accidentally failing to worship him in the right way as he would for killing someone. That comes, I believe, from giving more weight to a handful of passages rather than giving weight to the bulk of Scripture.

It seems to me, God brings down judgment primarily when people mistreat others and when they sit idly by and allow others to be mistreated. Over and over again, he tells his people that their religious ceremonies (even when carried out faithfully) mean absolutely nothing to him when they allow justice to be perverted under their noses. That isn't to say the religious ceremonies were unimportant, but they were less important to God than how people treated their neighbor.

But in a nation, like Israel or Judah, where justice is being perverted, idols are being worshiped, and sexual immorality is running rampant, everyone is defiled. Every person in the nation is stained with sin. God knows the difference between the righteous and the wicked, but the sins of the wicked have even defiled the righteous and they all suffer the consequences of sin together.

Death comes to them all, without distinction. Israel and Judah are massacred, carried off into captivity, and scattered all over the earth. Their punishment isn't some spiritual separation from God. Their punishment isn't described in terms of the afterlife. It is the here-and-now, they suffer and die because the land, the earth, and their own hands are polluted by sin. They are a cursed people. All the nations of the earth are cursed people.

The Promise of a Golden Age

Throughout these prophetic books, there is a promise of a new golden age for Jerusalem. It will be a time of peace and prosperity. A time when the nations of the earth will come to the people of Israel and be joined together into a single people. A time when there will be no more conflict or war. A time when justice and righteousness will reign forever and ever.

We even see glimpses of a King who will come. Some call the coming king David, some call him "the Branch," and some refer to him in other ways. But the idea is that a King will come, who will separate the righteous from the wicked and lead God's people in following the Lord. Finally, the remnant of people who love the Lord will no longer have to suffer the consequences of sin.

The remnant of Israel, and people of every nation, will be filled with love and faithfulness. They will learn to do what is right. The land will yield its produce as it was in the Garden. And there will be peace.

Unfulfilled Promises

You might suppose the books of Haggai, Zechariah, and Malachi would be joyful books. After all, these are the books that cover the period after the return from exile. But these may very well be the saddest books of all. When the people return from exile, their hands are still stained with sin and everything they touch is stained with sin.

Even though a few Jews have returned and the temple gets rebuilt, the vast majority of Jews are dispersed all over the Persian Empire. The rag-tag group of refugees who have returned to the land is hardly the fulfillment of the grand promises God had made.

And so the people must continue to wait for their coming King, the curse to be lifted, the land to become like the Garden of Eden, their sins to be forgiven, their enemies to be defeated, and the nations to come to them seeking salvation.

And that's where the minor prophets leave us, waiting for the King.

JOB

The name "Job" means "hated" or "persecuted" and Job certainly becomes a persecuted man. This book is a different form of literature than any of the books we have covered previously. It is the first book of the final section, "The Writings" and it is a work of "wisdom literature." The author uses a poetic story to correct some misunderstandings and guide God's people in the path of true wisdom. So, let's consider a few important truths from the book of Job.

The Satan

This is the first time in our Bible reading we have come across the term "Satan," which means "Accuser." And it will be helpful if you dismiss the idea of a red, pitchfork-wielding, horned lizardman. The character known as "The Satan" in this book acts as a prosecuting attorney, who puts Job on trial. He is trying to prove that Job, and mankind in general, only serve God when it is beneficial for them to do so.

In other words, The Accuser's position is that Job does not really love God for God's sake. The Accuser believes as soon as Job isn't prosperous anymore, he will forsake God. The Accuser is trying to prove that Job only sees God as a means to an end.

The only way for that position to be proven or disproven is for Job to be put on trial. So God allows Job to be put on trial so that his loyalty and love will be shown to be genuine.

The Prosperity Preachers

As soon as Job's suffering reaches its height, Job's so-called friends show up. They have a very neat and tidy view of the world. They believe if you are good, good things happen; if you are bad, bad things happen. Good people always reap the benefits of good behavior and bad people always get what's coming to them. If someone is rich and prosperous, it is because he is a good person. If someone is suffering, it is because he is a bad person. This is their wisdom.

In fact, one of the friends makes an interesting statement. He says that serving God is really of no benefit to God, it is of benefit to the one serving. When you are serving God, you are really just serving yourself, he says. You do good things for God so that he will bless you. But these friends are actually proving The Accuser's point. They are saying God is a means to an end; serving God is just a means of attaining health and wealth.

As far as this "wise and understanding" jury is concerned, they believe the evidence is clear: Job has been found guilty and has been imprisoned in suffering until he learns his lesson.

The One on Trial

But Job feels like he has been imprisoned without a trial at all. He feels like the sentence has already been carried out, without him being able to speak in his own defense. Throughout the book, Job's only desire is to be given the opportunity to stand face-to-face with God and argue his innocence. He believes he would be acquitted, but God is unseen so there is no one to whom Job can present his case.

Job feels like this kind of thing happens more than the friends would like to admit. Faithful people, who serve God well, suffer and die without any legacy or memory. While at the same time, wicked people prosper and die in their old age with a long and glorious legacy left for their children. He feels like justice is being perverted all around him and things aren't nearly as neat and tidy as the friends proclaim. This is the wisdom of Job.

But what Job cannot see is that his trial hasn't ended. He hasn't been sentenced, he is being tried. Will his suffering cause him to curse God and die or will he be faithful until the end?

The Judge

In the end, God does show up on the scene. The wisdom of the friends has been heard, the wisdom of Job has been heard, and finally the wisdom of

God is heard. God tells Job and his friends that they are incapable of seeing how the world really works and it isn't their place to accuse God of wrongdoing.

Finally, Job is vindicated and acquitted. In spite of the fact that he had been confused and angry, he never lost faith in God. He was loyal to God in spite of the fact that he was suffering unjustly.

The Resurrection of Job

In the end, God made all the bad things come untrue for Job. He received the reward for his unfailing loyalty and love. But don't miss the point that I believe is a thread throughout the whole book. Throughout the story, Job keeps talking about the faithful who are buried in the dirt and eaten by worms. He says there is more hope for a chopped down tree than them. Even a chopped down tree can sprout and grow again, but a person who is dead is dead.

But are they? Is there really no hope for those who've gone down to Sheol? Isn't that the question of the whole Bible; the question answered by the Good News?

Because of Jesus, those who have been faithful even unto the point of death will be raised to live forever. They will be crowned with glory and honor. The reward is great for those who are willing to meekly and patiently suffer and be persecuted for righteousness sake. This is our time of trial. Will we be faithful or will we forsake God when things don't go our way?

Perhaps we hear a faint glimmer of resurrection hope in Job's words:

> *I know that my Redeemer lives, and at the last he will stand upon the earth. And after my skin has been thus destroyed, yet in my flesh I shall see God, whom I shall see for myself, and my eyes shall behold, and not another.*

PROVERBS

Proverbs doesn't seem like the kind of book that is made for reading straight through in one sitting, or in one day. It seems like the kind of book which lends itself reading a few verses until you find one that "speaks to you." Though I don't think it was necessarily meant to be read in one sitting, there are some incredibly valuable insights that can be taken from considering all the proverbs as a whole.

Uncommon Sense

There are plenty of individual proverbs that any person can pull out of the book and say, "See, I do this. This is how my parents and grandparents taught me to live. It's just common sense." Some will pull out passages about:

> hard work
>
> discipline
>
> individual responsibility
>
> sobriety
>
> moral uprightness

They will say, "See, the Bible is full of practical instructions about how to be successful. Just work hard and take care of your responsibilities and you'll get along well in life."

But others will focus on proverbs that promote:

>social justice

>responsibility for the poor

>speaking up for the oppressed

>equity for all people

They will say, "See, the Bible teaches us to live modest lifestyles and give away much of our time, resources, and possessions to those who are disadvantaged."

Both of these viewpoints are incredibly common. You can find millions of people who are in one of these two camps. This is what you call "common sense" or common wisdom. It is the wisdom of just looking around and seeing how the world works and saying, "I think people ought to live this way," and then finding Bible verses that support our particular view point. That is incredibly common.

What is uncommon is the person who holds all of these truths in his or her heart simultaneously. After all, when was the last time you met someone who was equally concerned about moral uprightness as social justice? That is the uncommon wisdom of Proverbs and it is uncommon because it is spiritual and not worldly. A person with worldly wisdom sees half the truth and holds on to that half for dear life. A person with wisdom from above is willing to embrace the whole truth.

Stop Being a Fool

I used to read through the book and find proverbs that simply reinforced what I was already doing and think to myself, "It's other people who are fools. If they would just straighten up, the world would be a better place." But then I let the proverbs convict me and reveal to me that I am the one who has been foolish. I have not been upright, righteous, or wise. I have been the fool.

But over and over again, the proverbs make the point that you don't have to keep being a fool. You can learn. You can accept correction. You can humble yourself. You can ask for forgiveness and find God's mercy.

The upright and wise are not perfect people. They are people who accept God's correction and repent of their foolish ways. Just because you've acted foolish doesn't mean you have to keep living a foolish life.

Hopeful, Not Practical

It's also obvious that the book of Proverbs teaches that if you live an upright, righteous, and wise life, things tend to work out well for you. So it is very easy to think the proverbs are simply teaching us to live well because it is "practical" to do so. But from the beginning to the end, the message is that we should live well because it is pleasing to the Lord. The fear of the Lord must be the driving factor behind wise living.

Wisdom is knowing the will of the Lord and doing what pleases him. Consider the very import nuance between these two different types of people, who seem to be living very similar lives:

> One person is motivated to do good because he loves and fears the Lord, and his actions end up benefiting his own life.

> Another person is motivated to do good simply because he is seeking the benefit it will bring to himself.

It seems to me, the first man is painted as wise and the second is painted as foolish. Those who do the Lord's will very often prosper; but there is a vast difference between those who do the Lord's will because they fear the Lord and those who do it just because they are just seeking to prosper. The second type of man will eventually come to ruin.

When people turn the book of Proverbs into a book of pragmatic advice, sort of an ancient book of life hacks, they are totally missing the point of the book as a whole. The book is promoting wise living as defined and motivated by the Lord.

As Christians, it is our hope, our confident expectation, that all who put their trust in the Lord, even if they died in poverty and shame, will be raised in honor and glory at the coming of Lord Jesus Christ. That is the wisdom that the world finds foolish. That is the wisdom of the Spirit (see 1 Corinthians 2).

So, we do good not because we are trying to maximize our pleasure and minimize our pain; we do good because we fear the Lord. The result is the best possible life now, and also an unimaginably great life in the age to come.

RUTH

It would be easy to see the book of Ruth as a love story: A beautiful young woman, who has tragically lost her husband, meets a rich, handsome, and godly man who marries her and they live happily ever after. But that's a modern fairytale, not a biblical story. Romance and beauty are important themes in our stories, but the important themes in this story are things like showing kindness to the dead and caring for destitute immigrant workers and widows (things many Christians hardly think of as important themes).

Where It Fits in the Story

If you read the books of the Bible in their modern Christian order, then you would read the story of Ruth between Judges and 1 Samuel. This makes sense because the story occurs "in the days when the judges ruled." However, the problem with this order is that it interrupts the big-picture story of how God brought Israel into the garden of the promised land, they disobeyed and were exiled, but eventually returned to wait for their Savior-King.

But when you read the Bible in the TaNaK order, you read the big-picture story in the Torah and the Prophets, and then come back and read some of the "Writings," which help fill in some gaps as well as give wisdom and understanding.

The story of Ruth proves to be an origin story for King David. And knowing what we know about where the story is headed, this story fills us with hope that if God could bring David's family back from the brink of destruction once, he could certainly do it again. After the Babylonian exile, the family of David was like a tree stump, but a branch would grow from it again.

Kindness to the Living and the Dead

When Naomi and Ruth arrive in Bethlehem, they are two destitute widows. Ruth is an immigrant from a country despised by Israelites. And life has been so hard on Naomi that her friends in town don't recognize her. She is now a "bitter" old woman. She believes God is against her and that she will die in squalor.

But perhaps the worst tragedy of all is that her husband's family had been "cut off" from Israel. When a man died, he took comfort knowing he would live on through his children. That's why if a man died without having in any children, it was his brother's duty to marry his wife and have a child in his place. Through that child, the name of the dead would be perpetuated and he would live on through his offspring.

Naomi's husband had two sons, but both sons died without having any children of their own. So it wasn't that Naomi was just sad that she didn't have grandchildren to bounce on her knee. It's so much more than that. Her family's name had been cut off because there was no offspring through whom her husband and sons could live on.

That's where Boaz comes into the picture. He is a man who keeps the Law. Not because he "has to," but he keeps it from his heart. He allows poor immigrants to glean in his fields, he protects vulnerable women, and he provides for widows. He practiced the words of Moses from Deuteronomy 24:17-19,

> *You shall not pervert the justice due to the sojourner or to the fatherless, or take a widow's garment in pledge, but you shall remember that you were a slave in Egypt and the Lord your God redeemed you from there; therefore I command you to do this. When you reap your harvest in your field and forget a sheaf in the field, you shall not go back to get it. It shall be for the sojourner, the fatherless, and the widow, that the Lord your God may bless you in all the work of your hands.*

Boaz was a man of "justice," as the Bible defines justice. He showed kindness to Ruth, the sojourner, and to Naomi, the bitter old widow. He also showed kindness to Naomi's dead husband and Ruth's dead husband. He perpetuated their name. Because he was their relative, he was able to marry Ruth and have a child for the family in the place of the dead. In a sense, he brought the whole family back from the dead.

RUTH

Redemption

Much of this story centers around Boaz being a "redeemer," and I think we struggle a bit to understand redemption. In Israel, if someone fell on hard times, he could sell his portion of the Promised Land, but he and his family still had a perpetual claim to that plot of land forever. Even if he lost it for awhile, he or his relatives still had a right to reclaim it if ever they were financially able (or a year of Jubilee came around).

At the beginning of the story, because of a famine, Naomi and Elimelech sold their land near Bethlehem and move to Moab to be sojourners. Such a move would have felt like an exile. Perhaps they believed at some point they would be able to save up enough money, and after the famine had subsided, they would return to Bethlehem and reclaim their property. However, Elimelech and his sons died before that could happen. Naomi had nothing and no hope of ever buying back the family land.

When the story tells us Boaz became Naomi and Ruth's "redeemer," it is because, as a close relative, he had the legal right to buy back the family plot, restoring Elimelech's land to his family.

When we think about Jesus (the descendant of Boaz) being our redeemer, we should think in very similar categories. As human beings, we were exiled from our place in the Garden, but Jesus has "redeemed" us. He has reclaimed for us our inheritance, our place in the paradise of God near the tree of life. Through Jesus our redeemer, exile, bitterness, desperation, and hopelessness are coming to an end. He has spread his wings over us and has showed kindness to both the living and the dead.

Turns out, the book of Ruth is a love story…just a very different kind of love story.

SONG OF SOLOMON

Song of Solomon is a unique book of the Bible. It is love poetry. In fact, when the metaphors are properly understood, it is very sexually explicit. But why should such a book be in the Bible? Why is it important for God's people?

Wisdom Poetry

Like Proverbs or Ecclesiastes, the Song of Solomon is wisdom literature. It really helps to think of it in that light. It is included in our Scripture collection, not because it is about one particular relationship, but because it is about one particular kind of relationship. It is a book about a sexual relationship between a husband and wife.

There is a phrase used multiple times in the book, "awaken and stir up love." I've been thinking about that phrase and about the wisdom of those words. The bride in the story makes the women of Jerusalem promise not to awaken or stir up love until it is time. Presumably, she knows it is unwise to stir up her sexual desire for her betrothed before those desires can be consummated. Once they are married, however, her love should be awakened and stirred up for her beloved.

SONG OF SOLOMON

Metaphors About Love

The metaphor that love is something which can be stirred up and awakened, is incredibly helpful. But consider how it is in conflict with the way our culture thinks about love and sexual desire.

In our culture, we see love as something into which, or out of which, a person simply "falls." We talk about "falling in love" and "falling out of love." We think of it as something that just happens, like tripping and falling into a hole on the ground. "I fell in love," we say, "I didn't plan to, it just happened." Or, we say something like, "Over the years, we just sort of fell out of love with each other." This is a metaphor for love that we have allowed to shape our thinking and our behavior.

Another way people in our culture think of love is like two magnets. We talk about "attraction" like there is a strong invisible force that pulls people together. This is another metaphor that has shaped our thinking and our behavior.

But the poetry of Song of Solomon invites us to change our metaphors about love. This poetry pictures love like a part of us that is either awake or asleep. A person's love can be awakened with certain thoughts and ideas. Like waking up from a deep sleep, it happens gradually as those thoughts call out to love, "Wake up! Wake Up!" And by keeping those thoughts away, like a sleeping baby, love can be allowed to stay in a dormant state.

This would mean that instead of thinking, "I am very attracted to that person" (as if you were one magnet and they another), you might say, "My love for them is being awakened." Then, in light of that revelation, you must decide whether or not it is wise to allow your love to continue to be stirred up for that person. Or instead of thinking, "I have fallen in love with that person," you might think, "My love has been stirred up," and you must decide whether or not it is wise for your love to remain stirred up for that person.

Sexual Morality

Of course, when we think about love in this way, it helps us to understand that love can be stirred up for various people. In our culture we have all kinds of labels for people's sexual proclivities and preferences. We tend to believe that "heterosexual males" are simply "attracted" to females. That's just how it works, we think.

But the reality is, I should not be "attracted" to every female in the same way. I should not "fall in love" with random women, just because I am a "heterosexual male." I should awaken love for my wife and not allow love to be awakened for anyone else. And that is what the Song of Solomon is all about.

This book helps us understand God's will for human sexuality. A man should allow his love to be stirred up and awakened for the one woman to whom he commits himself in marriage; and a woman should allow her love to be stirred up and awakened for the one man to whom she commits herself in marriage. Love for other people should not be awakened; and even love for that particular person should not be awakened until marriage.

It seems possible for just about anyone's love to be stirred up toward anyone else, if you allow it to be; if you entertain thoughts and ideas to awaken those feelings of love. And, conversely, it's possible to allow a love you feel for someone to go to sleep if you do not keep those feelings of love awake.

Faithfulness in Marriage

Finally, one thought about the role of Song of Solomon in marriage. This poetry isn't just about a particular set of lovers. It's about any husband and any wife. These are the thoughts a husband ought to entertain about his wife and the thoughts a wife ought to entertain about her husband, in order for love to be awakened and stirred up. That's why this book is not pornographic, because it is not a picture of someone else. It's a picture of your spouse.

Every husband ought to think of his wife as the most beautiful and glorious woman in all creation. And every wife ought to think of her husband as the pinnacle of manhood. The wisdom of this book will help you entertain the kinds of thoughts that will keep love awakened for your spouse and only for your spouse.

ECCLESIASTES

Some books of the Bible are obviously easier to read in one sitting than others; and the extent to which doing so is beneficial varies from book to book. But some books of the Bible simply cannot be understood if they are read piecemeal. Some books must be read in one sitting and when read in one sitting the meaning is clear. The book of Ecclesiastes is a book like that. Pulling a passage out of context in this book almost guarantees missing the point of that passage.

The Circle of Life

One theme in the book is that from the human perspective, life seems circular. Everything just seems to go around and around in a big meaningless circle. Everything that has happening now, has happened before and will happen again. No progress has been made or will be made.

Kingdoms rise and fall. Generations come and go. People are born and people die. From the human perspective, the world is like a never ending merry-go-round. You get on and take the same trip everyone else has taken and then you fall off, just like everyone else, but the merry-go-round keeps spinning and spinning forever.

The only two constants for the Preacher of Ecclesiastes is the earth and the Lord. Everything else is just transitory and circular. Everything else is born to eventually die. Everything is going through the same meaningless cycle day after day, year after year, generation after generation.

Who Has the Advantage

The Preacher explores why it is just an illusion that some people have an advantage over others in life. From the human perspective, it seems like wisdom, pleasure, strength, toil, or wealth might give you an advantage over others. If you learn enough, gather enough, are strong enough, or work hard enough maybe you can win at life.

But in the end, who wins? No one. At the end of every generation, everyone is dead. No one wins. No one survives. And no one is really remembered. All the stuff people accumulated for themselves is given to someone else who will squander it and waste it away.

In light of our impending death, all the pursuits of chasing after strength, pleasure, learning, and wealth all just seem like a monumental waste. All these pursuits are like chasing after wind, even if you ever caught it in your hand, you would still have nothing.

The World from God's Perspective

The parallel theme is that while from man's perspective, life seems circular and meaningless, God is above all of this. God sees the big picture. God understands that there is a timeline and the story is making progress to some end. The Preacher even says God has given man some inkling in his heart about this eternal timeline, this big picture, but man never lives long enough to understand it.

The only wise choice for man is to submit himself to God and obey God's commandments, because God sees the big picture and we don't. The Preacher understands that even though those who fear God will die and will end up in a grave just like everyone (and everything) else, but it is still worthwhile to fear God and keep his commandments.

But why it is worthwhile to fear God and keep his commandments, remains a mystery in this book. The Preacher just assures us God will take care of those who fear him and keep his commandments.

The Mystery Revealed

The book of Ecclesiastes is the perfect introduction to the Gospel. Ecclesiastes explains the world from man's perspective, and then the Gospel reveals God's perspective. In the Gospel, God pulls back the curtain and shows us the big picture. God shows us what he has been doing from beginning to end.

ECCLESIASTES

Right now, everything is in bondage to corruption. Everything, including our bodies, is wearing out and dying. The whole creation is stuck in this seemingly endless cycle. Every single person knows, if he is honest, that what has happened to everyone else will happen to him, he will die.

But the Gospel invites us to put our faith in Jesus and look forward to the new creation, the point in time that the cycle of birth and death will be no more. Someday Jesus will return and bring the merry-go-round to a halt. Jesus will raise everyone from the dead, and those who belong to him will live forever as part of the new creation. The Gospel teaches us that the old things are all passing away and everything is being made new.

Ecclesiastes invites us to consider that we are wasting our short little lives chasing after the wind. Jesus invites us to stop wasting our lives. He offers to deliver us from this cycle of death. He invites us to devote our lives to following him and promises to give us life in the age to come, an age without death.

It's a beautiful thing to read Ecclesiastes in light of the Gospel.

LAMENTATIONS

Jerusalem was more than a city, it was a symbol. It was a symbol that this was the place on earth where God lived with his special, elect, chosen people. But because of Israel's cumulative sin, over the course of generations, one generation had to endure the destruction of the once great city. These songs are hard to read, they talk about people being murdered, women being raped, and children being cannibalized; but it's a pivotal moment in the story of the Bible and one every Christian must understand.

It's Not About You

The way we tend to read the Bible today really frustrates me. We read a passage, like Lamentations, and then we jump right to a personal application of the story. See if this sounds familiar: "God punished people for their sin, but he still loved them no matter what. Has there ever been a time when God let you endure the consequences of your sin? But be sure, God still loves you no matter what. Things will get better for you soon." That's really easy to do, but I do not think it's a helpful way to read the Bible.

The author of Lamentations is singing terribly sad songs about the fact that the people of Jerusalem are bearing the sins of their fathers. Each individual is not just suffering for his or her own personal sin, but for the sins of previous generations. The punishment for all of the injustice, the rebellion, and the idolatry is falling on this particular generation. From the perspective of the author, it looks as if God might very well be done with his chosen people.

Resist the urge to allegorize the text and make it a metaphor about your personal life. Understand that it is part of an epic story into which you will eventually fit, but it is specifically about Jerusalem's dashed hopes and dreams. God has left his people to starve to death in the streets, because they have rejected his kingship. What happened to all humanity in Eden, has now happened to the people of Jerusalem; the city has been exiled to suffer under the reign and rule of death.

A Few Verses of Hope

There are moments in Lamentations when the reader thinks there is no hope. The author seems to believe God might never forgive and restore this people back to their honored place. This is how the book ends:

> *Restore us to yourself, O Lord, that we may be restored! Renew our days as of old—unless you have utterly rejected us, and you remain exceedingly angry with us.*

But right in the middle of the book are the most beautiful words of hope, words of confident expectations that God will heal this broken place:

> *I call to mind, and therefore I have hope: The steadfast love of the Lord never ceases; his mercies never come to an end; they are new every morning; great is your faithfulness. "The Lord is my portion," says my soul, "therefore I will hope in him."*

God's steadfast love, mercy, and faithfulness gives the author hope. In spite of how things look, in spite of the dead bodies strewn in the dust and the stones of the temple lying in ruins, God will once again show his steadfast love, mercy, and faithfulness to his people. This "portion" is all the author has left. He has no home, no food, no money, no land. The only thing he has to put his hope in is the character of God.

When Is This Hope Realized?

As we zoom out from this story, we should not think of this hope in God's "steadfast love" being realized in the return from captivity. When the Jews returned to Jerusalem and began to rebuild, they were continually harassed by their enemies of the land. After that, historically speaking, the Greeks, and then the Romans, enslaved and tormented them. Most importantly, it was only a small portion of the Jews who returned; most of them remained dispersed in the world.

The story of the Gospel is that Jesus is the one to fully and finally take all of this sin upon himself. Not just Israel and Judah's sin, but humanity's sin.

LAMENTATIONS

Jesus drinks the cup for all the nations. And because he does this, the exile finally ends. The curse is finally lifted.

Jesus coming, dying, and being raised from the dead to bring the kingdom, is God keeping his promise to be faithful, to show his steadfast love, and to show mercy. In Jesus, God is showing his faithfulness to the people of Jerusalem, to the lost sheep of Israel, and to all the descendants of Adam.

The author of Lamentations was right to look beyond the destruction and put his hope in God's steadfast love. Though it took hundreds of years, God certainly did not disappoint. This particular author and all those like him, will be raised from the dead to live in peace and righteousness in the kingdom forever and ever.

Learning to Lament

Before I close this chapter, I feel compelled to say, Christians today need to learn to lament. We need to learn it's ok to admit the stark reality of our circumstances. It's ok to admit that we hate the way things are in our present evil age. Personally, I hate things like cancer, war, human trafficking, rape, abortion, suffering, child abuse, and death itself. I hate these things!

We need to stop trying to find the "silver lining." We need to stop downplaying things. We need to admit how much we hate them. We need to sing songs and recite poetry about how much we despise these things. This isn't being morbid or pessimistic. It is being realistic and biblical.

But in the midst of our lament, we must not forget to praise God and put our hope in him. Jesus gives us the hope, the confident expectation, that all of these things are coming undone and in the age to come they will be no more. We know for sure the steadfast love of the Lord never ceases and his mercies never come to an end, so we hope and rejoice in him.

But hope only makes sense, it only works as a bright light, if we are willing to be honest about the darkness. If we continue to act like there is no darkness, then what good is hope to us? Let's learn how to lament. Let's learn how to hope.

ESTHER

The book of Esther is an amazing story. There is even a Jewish holiday that has been celebrated for over 2,500 years, which commemorates the events of this story. But, unfortunately, many of us have a tendency to reduce this story to a moral parable, focusing on just one phrase, "Who knows whether you have not come to the kingdom for such a time as this." There is so much more to this story than that.

The Setting

The Persian King, Cyrus, allowed Jews to begin returning to Jerusalem around 538 B.C. The story of Esther takes place more than 50 years after that. Some Jews had retuned to their homeland, but most remain scattered and dispersed all over the Persian Empire. They are vulnerable and unprotected, still exiled all over the world because of their sin.

In the first chapter, we are told King Ahasuerus threw a drunken feast that lasted for nearly six months. Queen Vashti, refused to allow herself to be paraded in front of the drunken guests for their viewing pleasure. So she was deposed.

The king then did an unspeakably horrible thing, though we usually gloss over it. Upon the advice of his counselors, the king rounded up all the beautiful virgins in the Empire and claimed them for his own, adding them to his harem. One by one, he robbed each of them of their virginity until he found one he wanted to make his queen. This is the horrible process by which Esther, a beautiful young Jewish girl, found herself to be queen of the Persian Empire.

Esther didn't ask for this situation. She didn't apply for a beauty contest. This isn't a Disney fairytale. This is a situation where a tyrant took anything he wanted from his kingdom, doing whatever he pleased with them, because he believed his subjects were his property.

Winning Favor

A subtle theme that you can pick up in Esther's story is one which is also found in the stories of Joseph, Daniel, Samuel, and even Jesus. God helped these people gain favor in people's eyes. They have certain opportunities presented to them and are able to rise to positions of power and leadership because God caused people to look with favor upon them.

Esther is little more than a slave, but she is able to rise to a place of power because God (though he is not named) causes people to look with favor upon her.

Exile Ethic

Another theme in the story of Esther is that of selective disobedience to the Persian government. Mordecai, the man who raised Esther from a child, disobeyed the law when he refused to bow to Haman. His stated reason for this disobedience was simply that he was a Jew.

It isn't that Mordecai was subversive or rebellious. At one point, he even saved the king's life from an assassination attempt. But Mordecai made it clear, he was not a Persian. Though he accepted his situation and his role as a subject of Persia, his loyalty was to his own King, not to Persia.

Mordecai, it seems, was still following the instructions of Jeremiah, which had been written to the exiles long ago. Jeremiah told them to make their homes in exile and seek the welfare of the cities in which they were exiled. To be lights in those communities. But someday God would gather his scattered people back home in the days of the coming Messiah.

Esther was also persuaded to break the law, when Mordecai convinced her to intercede on behalf of her people. She was forced to decide whether she would silently try to pass herself off as a Persian, in order to save her own life, or take her rightful place with the Jewish people even though it meant breaking the law by approaching the king in court.

The exile ethic is not to be rebellious or subversive. It is to remember we are not citizens of the kingdoms, nations, and empires in which we live. It is to remember not to give our allegiance to these empires. It is to accept the consequences, even death, for being an unusual people dispersed in the world; a people who do unbelievable good and selfless things for the kingdoms in which they live, but belong to another kingdom.

The Primary Theme

With all of that said, I think the primary theme of Esther is this: God will always raise up a deliverer to save his people. Most of the Jews in the story are helpless. The only thing they can do is wear sackcloth and pray. None of them are in positions of authority to stop the coming slaughter of the Jewish people.

The point of the story is not that we are all in a position to do something great. The point of the story is that sometimes we are not in a position to do anything at all except pray and trust God. Mordecai believed that even if Esther refused to be the person by whom deliverance came, relief and deliverance would come from somewhere.

God would keep his promises. God would deliver his people. God would raise up someone to be a Moses, a Joshua, a David. In this case, the person God raised up to deliver his people from death was Esther. Consider how this points forward to Jesus:

1. God raises up a savior.

2. She gives her life selflessly, on behalf of her people.

3. Through her willingness to die for others, God's enemies are defeated and God's people are given life and honor.

4. She is vindicated and honored.

Like the Jews of Esther's day, we are dispersed throughout the world. We are often vulnerable and persecuted because our allegiance is to a kingdom without walls or armies. But we believe God has raised up a deliverer. He has selflessly given himself on our behalf. Through his sacrifice, God's enemies are being defeated and we will be given life and honor through him.

Trust in the Lord. He always delivers his people; even from death.

DANIEL

The book of Daniel is filled with several familiar scenes: the lion's den, the fiery furnace, and the hand writing on the wall. But do we understand the main point of the book of Daniel? Perhaps no other book of the Old Testament is more explicit about the coming Messiah and the role of God and his people in the world.

Being an Exile

Can you imagine a foreign empire attacking your city, arresting many of the city's people, and then deporting them to a far away place? As we've noted in several chapters, that is what happened to the people of Jerusalem. Babylonian troops marched into the city and humiliated the Jews. They chained up many people and took them off to be slaves. Many of these captives were very young, including Daniel and his friends, Hananiah, Mishael, and Azariah.

The goal of the Babylonians was to conform young men like Daniel to the Babylonian lifestyle. They wanted these men to talk, dress, eat, worship, and even think like Babylonians. They wanted them to forget about their homeland and their people, and give their loyalty to Babylon and her king, Nebuchadnezzar. Daniel and his friends would serve their captors diligently, but they would not be conformed. They would remain Jews, loyal to the God of heaven throughout the days of their exile.

The stories about Daniel and his friends gave the Jews a model of exactly how they should behave while living under an oppressive foreign government. Like Esther and Mordecai, these young men lived according to the exile ethic.

They worked hard, serving their captors without sedition or rebellion. They were above reproach; even their worst enemies struggled to find fault with them. They were respectful and submissive to the rulers over them. However, their true loyalty was to God and they would often disobey the laws of Babylon or Persia in order to be loyal to their covenant with God.

They accepted the penalty for their disobedience, even if it was death, because they trusted in God's power to save.

The first six chapters are different examples of when this exile ethic was lived out by Daniel and his friends and how every single time, God delivered them. That is a major theme of this book, God delivers those who humbly trust in him.

God is in Charge

Daniel served multiple rulers of Babylon. Then, Babylon fell to the Medes and the Persians and Daniel served multiple Medo-Persian rulers. He saw kings at the height of their glory and power, but also humbled and brought to their knees. In the visions he experienced, Daniel saw even more kingdoms and rulers rise and fall. In symbolic images, he saw the rise of rulers like Alexander the Great, Antiochus Epiphanes, and the Roman emperors. He knew they would do great and terrible things on the earth.

But the most important part of everything Daniel witnessed was that the God of his forefathers, the God of heaven, was in charge of it all. Every beastly empire would have to answer to God. God would allow them to rise and serve his purposes, but then he would bring them all to account. Every evil deed, every injustice, every drop of blood spilled would be brought before the throne of the Ancient of Days and he would judge righteously.

This truth, that God is in charge of kings and kingdoms, would be of great comfort to a people living under oppressive regimes for hundreds and hundreds of years to come.

The Messiah's Kingdom

God showed Daniel a secret, a promise that he would eventually send a King to establish a kingdom that would last forever. A kingdom that would never fall. This kingdom would start small, but eventually it would fill the whole earth. This kingdom would smash to pieces all the other kingdoms of the earth and it alone would stand forever with the Son of Man as its King.

Even the faithful who died would not miss out on this coming kingdom, they will be raised from the dead and shine like stars. You can hear, I'm sure, how Jesus borrowed the words we find in the last chapter of Daniel, "And many of those who sleep in the dust of the earth shall awake, some to everlasting life, and some to shame and everlasting contempt."

Daniel and those like him, exiled and dispersed throughout the world, would have to be faithful and patient, waiting for God's coming deliverance. But just as God delivered his people from Egypt, he would deliver this exiled people. He would forgive their sins, establish his Messiah's kingdom, judge every kingdom of the earth, raise the dead, and be with his people forever.

Living As Exiles Today

Though the Messiah has come and has finished his atoning work and his rule has been established, we continue to live as exiles, aliens, and sojourners in the kingdoms of men. We must continue to wait and be faithful. We must continue to strive to live our lives above reproach. We must not fear death. We must give our allegiance only to our King and his kingdom and pray, "Lord, come quickly."

EZRA-NEHEMIAH

Ezra-Nehemiah, two books that were originally one, were not written to give us management and leadership advice. They were not even meant as a collection of moral stories from the lives of godly men. When read them together in one sitting, Ezra-Nehemiah recounts a bitter-sweet chapter in the history of God's covenant people. It was a time that brought shouts of joy and tears of sorrow.

Brief Moments of Joy

When we think about Ezra-Nehemiah, we often focus on the positive moments. There were several moments of great joy in this story: Three waves of Jews returned to Jerusalem from exile. The foundation of the second temple was laid. Eventually, the new temple was finished.

Finally, the walls around the city were rebuilt and dedicated.

It took nearly one hundred years to accomplish all of this. There were many obstacles, setbacks, and opponents that slowed their progress, but finally the city was rebuilt and, "The joy of Jerusalem was heard far away." Even though there were many tears, there was also much shouting, singing, and praising God in this story.

God's Hand on Them

A repeated idea throughout Ezra-Nehemiah is that God's hand was on his people to protect them and give them success. As in the stories of Daniel and Esther, the people of God found favor in the eyes of pagan kings because God's hand was on them. There is no such thing as "good luck" or "good fortune" in this story. If something worked out well, it was because God's invisible hand was involved.

Throughout the exile, this remnant of God's people never lost hope. They never stopped believing God would keep his promise to gather all of his people from the nations and restore the land of Israel to them. Even though they knew God had been provoked to anger, he would one day forgive them and free them from their bondage. God had never stopped loving them, never stopped providing for them, and never stopped working his plan.

This hope led to obedience. Ezra and Nehemiah insisted that the Jews obey the Law of Moses, in hopes that their obedience would turn back God's wrath from them. This was a period of reform and rebuilding. They reinstituted the feasts and the sacrifices. They read and taught the Law to the people. They strictly enforced compliance. They tried everything they knew to turn the people back to God and turn away God's wrath.

Tears of Sorrow

But the wrath of God was not turned back in this story. Even though many Jews returned to Jerusalem and Judah, the exile had not ended. Both Ezra and Nehemiah use the word "slaves" to describe their state. They returned home in a state of slavery. These are the words of Ezra:

> *For a brief moment favor has been shown by the Lord our God, to leave us a remnant and to give us a secure hold within his holy place, that our God may brighten our eyes and grant us a little reviving in our slavery. For we are slaves. Yet our God has not forsaken us in our slavery.*

Every joyful moment in the story is followed by sorrow. Every triumph is followed by tears. Just when the reader thinks the sunshine is breaking through and the time of restoration was about to begin, another dark cloud would roll in and it would start to rain all over. When the temple's foundation was laid, there were young people shouting for joy and older people weeping in sadness. These words, on that occasion, seem to be the perfect commentary for this entire period, "The people could not distinguish the sound of the joyful shout from the sound of the people's weeping."

EZRA-NEHEMIAH

The Ezra portion of the story ends horribly, with Ezra trying to turn away God's wrath by sending away the foreign wives the Jews had married. He was appalled by the fact that Jewish men had taken foreign wives and he thought maybe if they abandoned their families, sending them away into the wilderness, God's wrath would be removed from them. Though this effort was sincerely motivated by a desire to do God's will, one wonders if Malachi (who lived and prophesied during this time) did not have this in mind when he wrote the words we find in Malachi 2:14-16:

> *The Lord was witness between you and the wife of your youth, to whom you have been faithless, though she is your companion and your wife by covenant. Did he not make them one, with a portion of the Spirit in their union? And what was the one God seeking? Godly offspring. So guard yourselves in your spirit, and let none of you be faithless to the wife of your youth. "For the man who does not love his wife but divorces her, says the Lord, the God of Israel, covers his garment with violence, says the Lord of hosts. So guard yourselves in your spirit, and do not be faithless."*

The Nehemiah portion of the story ends similarly. Nehemiah loses control. He screams and yells and curses at people. He threatens them, beats them, and even pulls out their hair. He is beyond frustrated. He is irate that the Jews continue to forsake the Sabbath, marry foreign wives, and dishonor the temple.

And the story ends. It ends in frustration. It ends with the people's hearts being unchanged. It ends with a dark cloud looming over Jerusalem. In spite of the progress made, the Jews are still in slavery.

Someone other than Ezra, Nehemiah, and the prophets would have to come to take away this curse. It would not be removed through tears, prayers, animal sacrifices, or sending wives away. It would have to be removed by the coming Messiah. Only he could lift the curse, free the captives, and redeem the people of God from exile.

CHRONICLES

When we read the Bible in the TaNaK order, the final book of the Old Testament is Chronicles; which, of course, our Bibles break into two separate books (1 and 2 Chronicles). I want to share why Chronicles makes so much more sense when it is read as the last book rather than reading it immediately following Samuel-Kings.

Two Contexts

When reading a historical narrative, like Chronicles, you have to consider the historical context of the story itself, but also the context of the audience for whom this story was written. Chronicles covers much of the same material as the books of Kings. However, the audiences for whom these books were written are different and therefore the stories themselves are different.

Kings was written to explain to exiled Jews why they were exiled and why they needed to repent. Chronicles, on the other hand, was written to Jews who had returned from exile to explain that God was merciful and willing to forgive their sins. The authors of these two different books may be covering some of the same events, but they cover them in very different ways, because they are writing in a different context with different motives.

The author of Chronicles assumes the reader is already familiar with the historical facts of the story. His goal is not just to relay the facts of what happened. His audience already knows what happened. His goal is to retell the story in such a way as to make a very important point. With wisdom from God's Spirit, he leaves out key details of the story, depicts historical figures in a slightly different light, and emphasizes different themes than the author of Kings. He is counting on his audience noticing these differences, because his point is being made by the different way the story is being told.

When you read Chronicles, you have to understand that the context of the story is after the decree of Cyrus that allowed Jews to start returning from Babylon to Judah. The original audience was asking themselves, "Does God still love us? Will he restore his kingdom to us?"

Notable Differences

The earlier book, the book of Kings, focuses on the history of both the Northern Kingdom of Israel and the Southern Kingdom of Judah, showing how both kingdoms "broke faith" with God and were exiled for their disobedience. However, Chronicles focuses only on Judah, mentioning Israel's history only when it intersected with Judah's history. The author of Chronicles is not concerned with the story of Israel's fall, his audience knows that story already. He is concerned with depicting Judah as a nation that has fallen but will rise again.

Another difference is the moral makeover David, Solomon, and others receive. David and Solomon are depicted in a much better light in this book than they are in Samuel-Kings. The author makes no mention of David's sin with Bathsheba or his murder of Uriah. Solomon's heart is not said to have been lead astray by his foreign wives; no mention is made of his idolatry at all. In fact, his Egyptian wife is mentioned just to point out the fact that Solomon insisted she live in her own house because the house of David was holy.

Little to no mention is made of the political power struggles and the division in Israel during the reigns of David and Solomon. Israel is said to have been "as one man" in their devotion to these kings. Of course, the reason for this way of telling the story is obvious. The author was reminding the exiles that another son of David would arise to lead all of Israel once again and that they should rally around him in loyalty and allegiance, just as they had with David and Solomon. This book focuses nearly all of its attention on the Kings who were descended from David.

One interesting theme in Chronicles is the connection between the king and the priesthood. The obedient and repentant kings of Judah focused much attention on appointing priests and making sure the temple was functioning as it was supposed to function. Again, it's not hard to understand why this is an important theme when we remember the context of this book's author and audience. The temple needed to be rebuilt and the priesthood needed to be reorganized. That's why it is so important to read Chronicles in conjunction with Ezra-Nehemiah.

God's Steadfast Love Endures Forever

I would have to say that the major theme of Chronicles is God's "steadfast love endures forever." There are so many examples and instances of kings and people realizing they have sinned, repenting of their sin, and seeking God's mercy. There are so many reminders that God's steadfast love for his people never fails.

The point was, if God's people will humble themselves and return to God, he would most certainly forgive them and restore the kingdom to them. Passages like the following encapsulate the theme of the whole book rather well:

> *If they sin against you—for there is no one who does not sin—and you are angry with them and give them to an enemy, so that they are carried away captive to a land far or near, yet if they turn their heart in the land to which they have been carried captive, and repent and plead with you in the land of their captivity, saying, "We have sinned and have acted perversely and wickedly," if they repent with all their mind and with all their heart in the land of their captivity to which they were carried captive, and pray toward their land, which you gave to their fathers, the city that you have chosen and the house that I have built for your name, then hear from heaven your dwelling place their prayer and their pleas, and maintain their cause and forgive your people who have sinned against you.*

When this book was written, the Jewish people needed reassurance that they were still God's people, God was willing to forgive them, God would still raise up a descendant of David to be their king, and God would bring back the scattered sheep of Israel and make them one people again.

Of course, as Christians, we know now God would do all that and more through his Anointed King, Jesus. However, these people would have to wait 400 years for that day to come. So, in the meantime, the Jews rebuilt the temple, appointed priests, taught the Law, and reminded themselves that God's steadfast love endures forever.

CONNECTING THE TESTAMENTS

Before we move on to the section of sacred writings we call the New Testament, we need to pause for a moment and recap what we have covered so far. I believe our ability to comprehend who Jesus is and what he accomplished hinges largely on how well we grasp the story of God and Israel prior to Jesus' birth.

Paradise and Exile

The story of the Bible begins with humanity in paradise, living in peace with God and all of creation. God, man, woman, animals, plants, and even the land itself are without enmity. Everything is in perfect harmonious relationship with everything else.

But when the serpent deceives Eve, she and Adam rebel against God, doing what he warned them not to do. They are cursed and banished from paradise. They no longer have access to the tree of life and are sentenced to die in a land of conflict. From this point forward, everything is out of harmony. God, man, woman, the animals, and the land, there is conflict between them all.

The story of Israel repeats this same narrative on a different scale. Abraham's descendants are brought back from an exile in Egypt and brought into a paradise. The paradise is described as a land flowing with milk and honey. But Abraham's descendants, just like their father Adam, did what God warned them not to do and were exiled from paradise.

The Old Testament story ends with Abraham's descendants having returned to the place of paradise, but not the condition of paradise. They had returned to Jerusalem, but the exile had not ended. Peace had not come. Conflict continued. They lived in the land, but it was not flowing with milk and honey. It was still, in many ways, "desolate and waste." The curse and stench of death remained.

Kingdoms of God and Kingdoms of Man

Another theme is that of kingdom. When we think of a "kingdom," we typically think of a realm where a king rules. However, in the biblical story, the theme is much more about the invisible rule of a king. When men rule, there is always corruption, oppression, and injustice. It is only when men humbly surrender to God's rule, that there is righteousness, peace, and justice.

Israel had the opportunity to live under God's rule. Or, to put it another way, Israel had the opportunity to live in the kingdom of God. But instead of living in the kingdom of God, Israel continually chose to return to living under man's rule. In the wilderness, after being delivered from Egypt, they longed to go back and live under Pharaoh's rule. During the period of the Judges, their rebellion led them to be oppressed by both Israelite and Gentile rulers. They begged Samuel to appoint for them a king like the other nations.

There is an undeniable desire humans have for wanting a strong military and economic leader to shepherd them. Humans feel weak and vulnerable without a king. Israel should have realized, of course, they didn't need a king of flesh because they had God as their king. But because Israel would not be content to live in God's kingdom, the Old Testament part of the story ends the way it began; with God's people as slaves to a foreign king. The king of Persia became, in a sense, the new Pharaoh. And after the Persian kings, there would be Greek kings, and then there would be Roman kings. Israel would be slaves to them all.

Even though many Jews were living in Jerusalem, they were not in God's kingdom. They were in the kingdom of man. They were ruled by a king of flesh. They awaited the son of David, a human king who would establish God's kingdom, God's rule, once and for all.

God's Faithfulness

The most important theme of the Bible is that God can be trusted. He always keeps his promises. He is slow to anger and abounding in steadfast love. If his people wait faithfully, they experience his deliverance and forgiveness.

In spite of the fact that the Jews had broken their covenant with God, their lack of faithfulness would not nullify his abundance of faithfulness. God would keep his promises to a remnant of them in spite of their rebellion.

And what were his promises? He promised to lift the curse and give his people the land. He promised to make his people into a multitude, like the stars in the sky. And finally, he promised to bless all nations of the earth through Abraham's seed. God's promises never changed from the time he made them to Abraham. He promised over and over again through the prophets that he had not changed his mind about the covenant.

At some point, a new generation would come along with whom God would renew his covenant. He would make final atonement for their sins and change their hearts, so they would sincerely do his will. To these, God would fulfill all the promises he had made. They would be the heirs of all of his Abrahamic promises.

The Story Doesn't Change

Please understand what I'm saying. I'm saying you cannot read these books of the Bible and think they are about how to live a good life and go to heaven someday. Nothing in these books gives the indication that "going to heaven" is even a minor theme, much less the major theme.

If we are going to understand the final era of the biblical story, the era of Jesus, we have to understand that Jesus didn't come to change the story, he came to fulfill the story. He didn't come to change the promises, he came to fulfill the promises. He didn't come to destroy the hopes of God's people, he came to fulfill their hopes. If Jesus really is the Messiah, the son of Abraham, the son of David, the son of God, then his followers will literally inherit all the promises God has made.

That, my friends, is what the next section of the Bible is all about.

MATTHEW

We have to remember when we read a gospel account, the author's intention is not just to relay the facts of what happened in Jesus' life. The author's intention is to organize the facts (and his own commentary on the facts) in such a way that the reader finishes the book with a certain impression about Jesus. It is as if the words and deeds of Jesus are various paints and the author, empowered by the Holy Spirit, has taken those paints and created a beautiful picture of Jesus.

The Kingdom of Heaven

The primary theme of Matthew's account is "the kingdom of Heaven." But what does "kingdom of heaven" mean? And what is the kingdom of heaven?

First, when we think of the word "heaven," we tend to juxtapose it with "hell." We often think of heaven and hell as a pair of contrasting words. Interestingly enough, the Bible does not pair those words like that. The Bible says a lot about heaven and a lot about hell, but not together.

When Scripture talks about "heaven," the word with which it is most often paired is "earth." Heaven is the space of God and earth is the space of man. The book of Matthew is all about Jesus bringing heaven's kingdom to earth. And remember, when we talk about kingdom, we mean "rule and reign." So, Matthew is painting a picture of Jesus as the one who has come to establish heaven's rule and reign on earth.

Another way to put it might be like this: Caesar brings Rome's rule, but Jesus brings heaven's rule.

One thing to notice is that the kingdom of heaven would be established during the lifetime of Jesus' contemporaries, but it would not be established in its fullness. The kingdom of heaven, according to Jesus' parables, begins small and inconspicuous and it grows over time. As the rule and reign of King Jesus continues to expand today, we could say the kingdom of heaven has come, is coming, and will come.

Jesus rules and reigns today, but not over all people. God's will is not yet done on earth as it is in heaven.

The Law and the Prophets

A sub-theme is that of the law and prophets being fulfilled. When we read the word "fulfilled," we shouldn't substitute it with, "done away with." Jesus didn't come to say you should no longer pay attention to Israel's Scriptures. In fact, the story of Jesus makes no sense without the background of Israel's Scriptures. Jesus is saying he is the climax and pinnacle of that story.

When Matthew says something Jesus did "fulfilled" a certain verse in the Old Testament, you should not for a moment think Matthew is pulling something "out of context." Nor should you think the Old Testament prophet was simply foretelling a specific event in the life of Jesus.

When you read, "This fulfilled what was written," you ought to go and read the chapter from which the quote comes. You will find that often the prophet being quoted wasn't speaking specifically about Jesus, but about Israel. Matthew is making the point that Jesus is the embodiment of Israel. Jesus is the living representative of the nation of Israel, the one who will fulfill Israel's covenant with God.

God as Father

Another theme is that God is Father. He is the Father of Israel; and specifically of Jesus, the perfect embodiment of Israel. Like the nation of Israel before him: Jesus was brought out of Egypt, brought through the wilderness, and was tempted and tested. However, unlike the nation of Israel, this Son of God was faithful to the Father. He did not fall away in the wilderness. He did the Father's will. And through Jesus, even Gentiles will be able to become part of the new Israel and experience the love and care of a heavenly Father.

The Sins of Israel

When we concluded the section on the Old Testament, we noted that the sins of Israel still loomed as a dark cloud over their heads. The people of God were still in exile, though some of them had returned to Jerusalem. 400 years later, Jesus finds them in the same predicament they were in during the days of Malachi. Jesus comes offering to forgive their sin and end the exile.

We tend only to think of sin as individual; and there is certainly a sense in which it is individual. But if we do not understand that sin is also cumulative, then we will never understand the story of Jesus. The generation in which Jesus lived finished filling up "the cup" of sin their forefathers started filling up. Killing Jesus was the final act of rebellion that sealed the fate of the wicked.

However, on behalf of all those who would put their trust in him, Jesus drank the cup. He absorbed the guilt, shame, and death of all the sins of humanity that had accumulated or would accumulate. For every individual who would become his disciple, they could return from exile.

But many would persist in sin. Jesus was driving out the evil spirit from Jerusalem, but that evil spirit would return with "seven other spirits more evil than itself, and they enter and dwell there." Jesus warned the wicked people of that generation that they would be shut out from the kingdom. They would be cast into the Valley of the Son of Hinnom (Gehenna). They were sacrificing Jesus, as their forefathers had sacrificed innocent sons and daughters of Israel, and their fate would be one of judgement.

Not long after Jesus warned them to repent of their wickedness, God sent Roman troops to Jerusalem. As Jesus predicted, "They destroyed those murderers and burned their city." The wicked people of Jerusalem who had long rejected the messengers of God and killed his son, were cast out into the darkness, where there was fire and weeping and gnashing of teeth.

Disciples of Jesus

The book ends with a proclamation that Jesus is God's anointed King with authority over everything in heaven and on earth. His disciples are sent out to the world to invite to the wedding feast as many they could find. Those who were originally invited rejected the invitation to be Jesus' disciples, but now the invitation has come to us.

Now we can be his disciples by being baptized and learning to obey all he commanded. Now we can have God as our Father. Now Jesus can be our

King. Now we can be part of God's mission of bringing the kingdom, so his will is done on earth as it is in heaven.

MARK

The books of Matthew, Mark, Luke, and John cover the same time period and recount some of the same details of Jesus' life, but each book is incredibly unique. One of the greatest mistakes Bible readers make is trying to combine the accounts and smooth out the differences. We tend to be very concerned with knowing the order in which things happened, but the authors were more concerned with theology than chronology. We need to start appreciating the unique way in which each book is written.

Action

Mark focuses the majority of the book on the things Jesus did, rather than what he said. The book moves quickly from one event to the next. Jesus does one thing and then he is quickly moving to some other place and doing some other thing. It's actually hard to keep up sometimes.

Reading the book of Mark is a lot like watching an action movie. In fact, like many action films, the book of Mark begins with very little introduction to the characters, the setting, or the plot. If there isn't already some familiarity with the story, the reader would feel a little disoriented from the beginning. And I think, perhaps, that is part of the point.

Mark is not presenting a picture of Jesus that leaves the audience thinking, "What a lovely story. I will think about these things for a while. Perhaps someday I will follow Jesus." Rather, the book leaves the reader saying, "What just happened?! I've got to know more about this Jesus. If these things are true, the world is totally different now and I need to become a follower of Jesus immediately."

The first scene is that of John baptizing Jesus. As soon as Jesus is baptized, the heavens are "torn open." Notice the heavens do not gently open but are "torn open" (as the curtain in the temple will later be torn open). And when the heavens are torn open, the Spirit descends on Jesus like a dove. Mark leaves no doubt in our minds, heaven and earth are coming together in the person of Jesus in a powerful and action-packed way.

Cause and Effect

A person could not read the book of Mark and fail to notice his use of the word, "immediately." In the ESV, the word "immediately" is found 35 times in Mark's 16 chapters. Jesus says or does something and immediately something else happens. Or someone else says or does something and immediately Jesus responds.

It seems to me that it is all about cause and effect. The Son of God coming into the world has an immediate effect on the people with whom he comes into contact. There are some who immediately receive him and others who immediately reject him. When Jesus gives a command, the result is almost always immediate.

Which, of course, leaves the reader feeling as if he or she must respond to Jesus immediately. There is no time to delay. Heaven has been ripped open, healing and salvation are being offered.

Gentile Audience

One of the major differences between the book of Matthew and the book of Mark is the less frequent quotations from the Old Testament. Certainly, the story of Jesus remains distinctly Jewish and Jesus' claims must be understood in light of the story of Israel. But Mark does not seem to assume his audience is necessarily familiar with that story. In fact, several times, Mark parenthetically explains to the readers certain Jewish traditions or Aramaic phrases.

When Jesus cleansed the temple, he said, "Is it not written, 'My house shall be called a house of prayer for all the nations'? But you have made it a den of robbers." In Matthew and Luke's account, you will not find the words, "for all the nations." Mark is emphasizing the fact that the temple was always supposed to be a house of prayer for Jews, as well as Gentiles.

And as the book of Mark comes to an end, Jesus tells his apostles to "Go into all the world and proclaim the gospel to the whole creation." It isn't just Jerusalem and Israel that will be affected by Jesus' coming, but the whole creation. The curse is being lifted and all of Adam's descendants, both Jews and Greeks, need to hear about it. "Whoever believes and is baptized," Jesus says, "will be saved."

Now that's good news!

LUKE

Perhaps one reason I love the Gospel of Luke so much is that Luke was a traveling companion of the apostle Paul. So, Paul likely had a great deal of influence on how Luke's gospel was compiled. The themes Luke explores and highlights help us understand Paul's epistles even better. Some of the themes in this book might even surprise you.

Gentiles as Children of Abraham

Like the book of Matthew, Luke's gospel account quotes often from Israel's scriptures and makes reference to Israel's story. However, in Luke's account, there is an even greater emphasis on the fact that Jesus came to rescue people of every nation. In a way, Luke takes the heavy Jewish emphasis of Matthew and the heavy Gentile emphasis of Mark and weaves them together, showing that the Messiah came to offer redemption to the Jew first and also to the Gentile.

In the very beginning of the book, Luke records the words of four different Spirit-filled people who had waited their whole lives for the Messiah. Zechariah, Mary, Simeon, and Anna all testify to the identity and the vocation of Jesus. They speak of how Jesus would show mercy to the offspring of Abraham, save the offspring of Abraham from their enemies, cause the fall and rising of many in Israel, and relieve those who were waiting for the redemption of Jerusalem.

Luke talks more about Abraham than any of the other gospel accounts. It is obvious he wants the reader to understand Jesus came to fulfill the promises God made to Abraham's children. But to all those Jews who thought the Messiah would rescue them from the coming destruction of Jerusalem simply because they were descendants of Abraham, John the Baptist said:

> *Do not begin to say to yourselves, "We have Abraham as our father." For I tell you, God is able from these stones to raise up children for Abraham.*

The Jews who rejected Jesus were cut off from the family tree of Abraham and the Gentiles who put their faith in Jesus are grafted into the family tree of Abraham. That's the story Luke is telling. Like his friend Paul, Luke is teaching that anyone who puts their faith in Jesus can be considered Abraham's heir.

The Poor, Hungry, and Sick

Luke emphasizes Jesus' ministry to the poor and sick of Israel. Jesus not only ministered to the poor, but he also condemned the rich of Israel for neglecting their brethren. The reader should not think for a moment that "poor" or "sick" or "hungry" should be understood in metaphorical or symbolic terms. Jesus came to bring down the mighty from their thrones and exalt those of humble estate. He came to fill the hungry with good things and send the rich away empty. Jesus literally reduced poverty, hunger, and sickness in Israel.

But what does that mean for followers of Jesus today? First, it means we must obey the commands of our King. We must show the same kind of mercy to those in our global community as Jesus showed the people of his community. If we have food and clothing, we must share with those who do not. The kingdom of God must literally reduce poverty, hunger, and sickness in the world.

Second, Jesus was showing us what will happen "in the age to come" for all of his people: the sick will all be healed, the dead will be raised never to die again, the hungry will all be satisfied, and the poor will all be rich. Again, we come away with a very strange interpretation if we read terms like poor, hungry, and sick as metaphors or as symbolic language. Wherever the kingdom of God spreads, there should be tangible evidence and when the kingdom of God reaches its fullness, God will literally put an end to sickness, death, and poverty.

Rebuking the Powers of Darkness

Finally, there is a theme in Luke's account that I have often overlooked. Luke reveals the fact that the evil we can see, like poverty, sickness, anger, and murder are all the result of demonic forces working behind the scenes.

Throughout the book, when Jesus healed someone, he was breaking the demonic hold on that person and setting them free.

For instance, there was a woman Jesus healed on a Sabbath day. She was disabled, bent over and unable to straighten herself. Jesus called the woman a daughter of Abraham, who Satan bound for eighteen years. Jesus described healing her as loosing the bond Satan had on her.

When people do evil things, Luke helps us to understand they are unknowingly participating with the powers of darkness. Judas and the Jewish rulers partner with Satan to murder Jesus. When Jesus was arrested, tried, and executed it is as if the powers of darkness overwhelmed him and brought him down to the grave.

But as Jesus did throughout his ministry, he overcame. He rebuked Satan, the demons, and the powers of darkness. He was innocent of any crime, full of the power of God, with the authority to tread on serpents and scorpions. Therefore, the powers of death could not hold him in the grave.

The apostle Paul wrote that we become united with this very same power of God when we are baptized into Jesus (Romans ch. 5-6). When we put our faith in Jesus and are buried with him in baptism, Satan's grip on us is broken. We are delivered from the rule and reign of death, so that when Jesus returns we will experience the SAME sort of resurrection Jesus experienced. And not only that, Paul says Satan's grip on the entire creation will be broken and the whole creation will experience redemption (Romans ch. 8).

We aren't delivered from some sort of metaphorical or symbolic death. We are delivered from actual death. We will die, of course, just as Jesus died. But because we are declared innocent, because we are filled with God's Spirit, Satan has absolutely no claim on us. On the day of Resurrection, death will not be able to hold us either!

Praise God! Jesus has rebuked and defeated the powers of darkness on our behalf!

JOHN

Like the other gospel accounts, John's account is packed full of themes, concepts, and ideas. I couldn't possibly summarize them all. However, there are a few themes which stand out to me most prominently. If you pay attention to these, as you read through John's gospel account, I think you will clearly see the picture he is painting about Jesus.

John's Introduction

First, John makes it easy to understand what themes will be important in his account by including them in his beautiful introduction. In fact, you could read the first 18 verses of this book and have a pretty decent idea about everything that follows. He begins by identifying Jesus as the divine "word of God," through whom everything was created. This relationship between Jesus and God, his Father, is the major theme of the book. It is John's primary intention for his readers to believe that Jesus really is the divine Son of God.

But John also helps us to understand the condition of the world when Jesus arrived. The imagery of light and life versus darkness and death are introduced and then woven throughout the entirety of the book. Mankind was in utter darkness and dying until Jesus showed up as the light to bring life to the world.

Finally, in the introduction, the reader will notice that John's gospel account is unique. John definitely depicts Jesus as coming to his own people, but his concern is for the whole world. John helps us to see that Jesus' mission is about expanding the family of God far beyond Israel. Like all of the other gospel accounts, this book is deeply rooted in the history and promises of the Jewish scriptures, but it is probably the most universal in its scope.

The Role of the Spirit

Throughout the book, John makes a point of telling the reader that certain words and deeds of Jesus only made sense to the apostles after Jesus had been raised and glorified. They didn't immediately see the connection between what Jesus was doing and what was written in the Scripture. They only saw the connection in retrospect. After Jesus was resurrected and glorified, the apostles "remembered" and saw all of the connections.

This seems to be John's way of saying the Spirit of God was working in him and the other apostles as they retold the story of Jesus because Jesus told them the Spirit would help them do this very thing. The Spirit is the one who helped the apostles put all these pieces together, remember what happened, and see the connection between Jesus and the promises of Scripture.

In John's account, Jesus places a great emphasis on what the Spirit will do not only for the apostles but also for all believers. Jesus speaks of the Spirit like a river of living water that will flow into and out of the hearts of people, bringing them eternal life. This will change people in radical ways. It will bring people together and transform them into the sort of worshipers the Father seeks.

Light and Life

As was emphasized in his introduction, John continues to weave into his narrative the theme of Jesus being God's glorious light shining in a dark world. Those who allowed the light of Jesus to fall on them were transformed by Jesus' glorious presence. The recipients of the light became sons and daughters of light. When the "light of the world," returned to the Father from whom he was sent, the followers of Jesus were left to be light in the world.

The light brought life to humanity. When Jesus talks about "life," we should not suppose he means this in a philosophical or metaphorical sense. He means "life" in a similar way a doctor means "life." He means life, as opposed to death.

People in darkness die and Satan has claim to them. But those in the light are a different kind of human because Satan and the forces of darkness have no claim to those in the light. Those who believe in Jesus will die, but they will live again because Jesus is "the resurrection and the life." Jesus has the authority to undo death. He has the authority to call to those in the grave, "Come out!"

Jesus says when a person receives his light, they become possessors of a special kind of life, a life for the next age. The way this is expressed in our English Bibles is, "eternal life." The word translated "eternal" literally means "for the age." All those who are truly trusting in Jesus have received the gift of life for the age to come.

Sent From, Going To, and Coming Back from Heaven

The primary theme of John's account is that Jesus is from heaven. He has been sent to earth by God, who is his Father. It isn't as if John is unaware of Jesus' birth in Bethlehem or of his mother, Mary. Though John does not record the birth narrative, he makes reference to Jesus' family and especially his mother. He knows Jesus is fully human, but he also relates that Jesus is fully divine.

Not only was Jesus from heaven, sent by God, but his plan was to return to the Father. He made it very clear that the window of opportunity to bask in his light was short. But he also made it clear that in his absence, the ministry of the Spirit would make it possible for much more to be accomplished in his name. His followers, empowered by the Spirit, would continue to take light, life, and love to all humanity.

Jesus assured his followers they would see him again; not only his original followers but all of us who have believed because of their testimony. He tells us he is preparing a place for us in his Father's house and that he and the Father will come and make their home with us. And while we wait, we continue to encourage the world to "believe that Jesus is the Christ, the Son of God, and that by believing [they] may have life in his name." We encourage them to be born again by the water and the Spirit, to become sons and daughters of light.

ACTS

Growing up, I could probably quote more verses, and relate more stories, from the book of Acts than from any other book in the Bible. I thought I knew the book forward and backward. Unfortunately, the truth is, I had never even paid attention to the major themes. Some of the verses I memorized seem to me now to be more incidental details than key passages. So, what are the major themes of the book of Acts? What message was Luke conveying to his audience?

Acts as a Sequel

It's difficult, if not impossible, to understand Luke's message in the book of Acts unless you read and understand his gospel account. Both books were written to someone called "Theophilus," so we should expect the themes Luke began in the first book to be continued in the second book.

If you recall from our discussion of the Gospel of Luke, three of the major themes were: Gentiles can become children of Abraham; Jesus cares for the poor, hungry, and sick; and Jesus has authority to rebuke the powers of darkness. In that chapter it was noted, "Wherever the kingdom of God spreads, there should be tangible evidence and when the kingdom of God reaches its fullness, God will literally put an end to sickness, death, and poverty." And we also noticed, "The evil we can see, like poverty, sickness, anger, and murder are all the result of demonic forces working behind the scenes…when Jesus healed someone, he was breaking the demonic hold on that person and setting them free."

Both books are about Jesus waging war on Satan's kingdom, but that fact is often overlooked in favor of important, but elementary, teachings on how the early Christians did church.

Restoring the Kingdom of Israel

In the first chapter of Acts, the apostles asked Jesus, "Lord, will you at this time restore the kingdom to Israel?" I always thought their question revealed their misunderstanding about the kingdom. But as it turns out, the misunderstanding was mine.

Jesus spent the entire forty days between his resurrection and ascension, "Speaking about the kingdom of God." When the apostles asked about the timing of the kingdom, Jesus did not dismiss their question as if it were foolish. He promised they would receive power from the Holy Spirit. Through the apostles and the Spirit, the book of Acts describes how Jesus began in Jerusalem overthrowing the enemy who held his people in bondage.

The enemy wasn't Rome. Rome was just a visible symptom of the enemy's control. The real enemy, of course, was Satan. On the Day of Pentecost, Jesus brought thousands of Jews "from every nation under heaven" under the rule and reign of God. He set them free from Satan's grip. The book of Acts recounts how Jesus led his army of spiritual warriors on a battle campaign from Jerusalem to Judea and Samaria and then to the ends of the earth.

Everywhere the apostles went, by the power of the Spirit and at the name of Jesus, the world was being given back to God.

Amazed and Astonished

Luke constantly speaks of people being amazed, astonished, and in awe. He speaks of signs and wonders. Some truly amazing things happen in the book of Acts: The shadow of Peter, and objects Paul touched, were able to make sick people well; blind people were given sight; dead people were raised to life; demons were cast out; and poverty was eliminated in the Christian community.

All of these amazing and astonishing signs and wonders were evidence that Satan's grip was being broken and God's reign was being established. The visible manifestations of Satan's rule, division, war, poverty, sickness, and death are all threatened by the preaching of the name of Jesus. Satan's kingdom began to crack and crumble at the preaching of the apostles and someday his rule will be completely overturned.

The Jew First and Then the Gentile

Another theme Luke foreshadowed in his gospel account, which came to fruition in the book of Acts, was that the Jews' rejection of Jesus led to the offer of covenant membership being extended to the Gentiles.

In Luke 14, Jesus told a parable which can help us understand the entire book of Acts. In the parable, a man threw a great banquet and invited many guests, who rejected the invitation. These guests represent the Jews who rejected Jesus and rejected God's invitation to be part of his kingdom. Both in the book of Luke and the book of Acts, the Jewish leaders are constantly plotting to assassinate God's messengers (Jesus, Stephen, Peter, Paul). They hardheartedly refuse to listen to Jesus' invitation.

So, in the parable, the master sends his servant to, "bring in the poor and crippled and blind and lame" to the banquet. The servant does so but reports there is still room. So the master tells his servant:

> *Go out to the highways and hedges and compel people to come in, that my house may be filled. For I tell you, none of those men who were invited shall taste my banquet.*

In Acts, Paul is one of the servants who is tasked with compelling the world to "come in," so that God's house may be filled.

Jesus' Charge to Paul

I think it's fitting for us to conclude with Jesus' words to the apostle Paul about his mission. Jesus told Paul that he was sending him to both the Jews and the Gentiles, "to open their eyes, so that they may turn from darkness to light and from the power of Satan to God, that they may receive forgiveness of sins and a place among those who are sanctified by faith in me."

I think those words sum up the book of Acts (and the mission of the church today) rather well.

ROMANS

The main reason we misunderstand the Bible is that we are often asking the wrong questions when we read it. Imagine a boy in a chemistry class asking his teacher, "How do I find the subject and the verb in this chemical formula?" Or imagine a young lady in a history class asking her teacher, "How do I calculate the square root of the Emancipation Proclamation?" When you begin with the wrong sorts of questions, you will likely end up very confused. What questions should we be asking when we read Romans and what questions should we not be asking?

The Questions We Typically Ask of Romans

Christians today carry 2,000 years of religious baggage. Even those of us who want to think we approach the Bible with an open mind often do not realize just how much church history influences our thinking. Most of us are completely oblivious to the fact that our questions and assumptions are largely shaped by theological debates that raged centuries ago. The problem is, however, these theologians and religious leaders seem to have asked a lot of questions the biblical text wasn't trying to answer. Here are some examples:

> Do people have free will or does God determine each person's eternal destiny?
>
> Did Adam's fall cause his descendants to be born with a depraved sinful nature?

Does a person have to be baptized to be saved?

If we do not deserve salvation, how can we ever lose it?

These are not the sorts of questions the apostle Paul was addressing when he wrote his letter to Christians in Rome. Think back to the chapters Moses and the prophets. Are these the sorts of things they addressed? Did any of the Jewish Scriptures give us the impression this was the sort of conversation we were having?

Every book of the Bible has been concerned with God's relationship to the descendants of Abraham:

> He adopted them.
>
> He made a covenant with them.
>
> He made them fruitful and multiplied their numbers.
>
> He gave them the land of Canaan.
>
> Even after their sin and rebellion, he still promised through the prophets he would forgive all of their sins.
>
> He promised to restore the kingdom to them.
>
> He promised them a future of peace and prosperity.

These are the sorts of things the Bible has been about up to this point. Why would it suddenly shift and become just another religious manual about how to go to the good afterlife? That seems rather strange, doesn't it?

The Questions Paul Was Answering

In reality, Paul hasn't departed from the storyline of the Bible. He is still talking about the fact that all of these things belong to Israel: "the adoption, the glory, the covenants, the giving of the law, the worship, and the promises." In fact, one of the major questions he addresses in Romans is whether or not God has broken his promise to Israel. Has God been unfaithful? Has he rejected the Jews in favor of the Greeks?

Paul's answer to this is, Of course not! God has not been unfaithful and he has not rejected the Jews. God has created a new Israel by bringing both the Jews and the Gentiles into a covenant relationship with himself. All those who put their faith in Jesus are Israelites and all those who reject Jesus are not Israelites (even if they are physically descended from Abraham).

God has put together a new multi-racial and multi-ethnic people and there are all kinds of questions that come along with this arrangement:

> Should Gentiles be circumcised as a sign of the covenant?
>
> Should Gentiles observe the Sabbath?
>
> What sorts of food should followers of Jesus eat and avoid eating?
>
> Are Jews who follow the Law, but do not follow Jesus, part of the covenant family?
>
> If God is just giving away covenant membership as a gift, can we behave any way we want?
>
> Are Jews better than Greeks or are Greeks better than Jews?

These are the types of questions the book of Romans addresses. If you begin by understanding that Paul's primary point is about Jews and Greeks all being part of God's covenant people and heirs of the promises God made to Abraham, you will better understand this book.

Current State and Future Glory

There is a sub-theme I would also like to briefly address that often gets overlooked by modern readers. In this book, Paul talks about "Sin" as if it is a person rather than just something we do. This is a way of thinking about sin that is unfamiliar to many of us.

Paul speaks of "Sin" as if it is a horrible ruler who rules over both the Jews and the Gentiles. Every human being is a slave, laboring to do the will of "Sin." Every human has been condemned to work for "Sin" until they are finally killed. This death is their wage, their payment for being a slave of "Sin." Like the children of Israel laboring under Pharaoh in Egypt, all humanity needs a Deliverer.

Jesus, of course, becomes that deliverer for both Jew and Gentile. Paul explains that at baptism, both Jew and Gentile undergo a death and burial of sorts. Therefore, Sin's grip on each baptized person is broken, because they have died, been buried, and been raised up with Jesus.

But it is only the spirit of man that has been raised; the body is still weak and capable of being hijacked by Sin. Paul explains that the Spirit of God, who dwells in the body of every baptized person, will help us fight against Sin. Unfortunately, one day our bodies will die because of Sin, but, "The Spirit of him who raised Jesus from the dead…will also give life to [our] mortal bodies through his Spirit who dwells in [us]." Even our bodies will be redeemed from Sin's curse!

And as we wait for God's future glory to be revealed, we are called to love each other, love our neighbor, and love our enemy. As Paul writes, "Love does no wrong to a neighbor; therefore love is the fulfilling of the law."

1 CORINTHIANS

As we read through 1 Corinthians, it is vitally important for us to get an overall impression of the Corinthian church in our minds. We need to read the book from beginning to end and ask ourselves what life was like in the Corinthian church. Some of the problems the Corinthian church was dealing with are obvious, but other problems are more subtle. We have to pay close attention to context clues throughout the book if we want to understand this letter. Here are some of the problems in the Corinthian church and how Paul dealt with them.

Problems in Corinth

Some of the problems with the Corinthian church are obvious:

> division and quarreling
>
> sexual immorality being tolerated
>
> Christians suing each other in court
>
> chaos during the worship assembly
>
> misuse of spiritual gifts

These are just a few of the problems that were going on in this Corinthian church community, and you're probably aware that these problems existed in Corinth.

1 CORINTHIANS

However, there are a few underlying problems in Corinth that may only notice when we read the whole book from the beginning to the end. One of the major underlying problems is arrogance. There were people in Corinth who thought they were "spiritual" people. (That word "spiritual" is a keyword to this book.) These people believed they did not need to listen to the apostle Paul because of their superior spirituality. Paul spent the first several chapters explaining to them just how wrong they were.

These unspiritual people, who believed they were quite spiritual, were teaching things that weren't true and were tearing the church apart.

The Solution to the Problems

Paul's solution to these kind of problems was nearly always the same. He brought everything back to the core tenants of the Good News: the death, burial, and resurrection of Jesus. In fact, Paul reminded them of when he had been in Corinth, every bit of his teaching revolved around, "Jesus Christ and him crucified."

In the letter, Paul demonstrated how their sinful behavior was inconsistent with following a Messiah who selflessly gave himself up for others. He showed them how their behavior and their warped thinking were inconsistent with the belief that, "God raised the Lord and will also raise us up by his power." He brought everything back around to the cross and the resurrection.

This should be a lesson for us. The way we should encourage Christians to act like Christians is by preaching "Jesus Christ and him crucified." We have to bring everything back to the cross and the resurrection. If our thinking or behavior is inconsistent or incompatible with the cross and the resurrection, then we should abandon them immediately.

How to Form a Community of Jesus Followers

The book of 1 Corinthians is so incredibly valuable to us because Paul is reminding this church what a community of Jesus followers should look like. Consider some of the things he teaches them in this letter and how these principles would apply to us today:

> If we are spiritual, we will humbly listen to the teachings of Jesus' apostles.

> We should be unified in our common baptism.

It is imperative we follow the sexual ethic that was taught by the Law, upheld by Jesus, and commended to Gentile Christians by the Jerusalem council.

It is appropriate and necessary to remove people from our fellowship if they refuse to live a life consistent with the Gospel.

Disputes amongst believers should be handled internally, rather than taking each other before secular courts.

We must be careful we are not sending the wrong messages when we adopt the customs and practices of unbelievers.

We should be willing to give up our rights for the sake of one another's conscience.

The weekly assembly, when we share the Lord's Supper, should be well-organized, edifying, and Christ-centered.

The greatest spiritual gift is love, without which everything else is meaningless.

Paul was concerned with the Corinthians' behavior inside and outside of the weekly assembly. In many ways, it seems he wanted the church community to function similarly to the way the Jews' synagogue was supposed to function. He wanted the Christian community to be a beacon of truth and love within the city of Corinth and he wanted his brothers and sisters to have the structure, encouragement, and support of a loving spiritual community. Obviously, we should strive to create similar types of Christian communities today.

The Resurrection of the Dead

It is interesting that Paul spends a great deal of time at the end of this letter dealing with a particularly troubling false teaching. There were apparently people in Corinth teaching that there would not be a bodily resurrection. It isn't that these people did not believe in an afterlife, but they did not believe in a resurrection. We seem to have many modern Christians who have accepted this lie as well.

Paul emphatically taught that if there is no bodily resurrection, then Christianity is a lie and no one should be a Christian. The bodily resurrection of Jesus and the coming resurrection of all people is at the very heart of Christian teaching. It is why we believe and do everything that we do.

He explains, of course, that our resurrection body will be "spiritual," but that doesn't mean it will not be physical. Notice that Paul does not contrast "spiritual" and "physical," he contrasts "spiritual" and "natural." He says these current bodies of ours will be raised from the dead and transformed by spiritual power from heaven. Because of the power of the Spirit, our bodies will be transformed to be immortal and imperishable.

Again, to the apostle Paul, this coming resurrection was key for much of his teaching. As we noted earlier, even his teaching about sexual immorality was anchored in the fact that our body is meant for the Lord, because "God raised the Lord and will also raise us up by his power."

Jesus has been raised and we will also be raised when that final enemy, death, is destroyed and we live with God and his people forever and ever.

2 CORINTHIANS

The apostle Paul's follow-up letter to the church in Corinth starts off very meek and mild. However, in the second half of the letter, his tone changes and he deal directly with the primary problem in Corinth. The primary problem in Corinth is that there are people undermining Paul's authority and credibility. Second Corinthians is such a relevant book for Christians today because there are still many who undermine Paul's authority and credibility.

What Paul's Critics Were Saying

It seems the majority of Christians in Corinth were supportive of Paul's ministry and submissive to his apostolic authority. When he wrote to them about their sins, they were sorrowful and repented. However, there were others who were being led astray by Paul's critics. Here are some of the things the critics were saying about Paul:

> He wronged, corrupted, or took advantage of people.
>
> He walked according to the flesh.
>
> His letters are weighty and strong, but his bodily presence was weak, and his speech of no account.

The men who were saying such things were also claiming they worked "on the same terms" as Paul. They apparently boasted of themselves, their authority, and their ability. They claimed to have apostolic authority, but Paul called them:

- False apostles
- Deceitful workmen
- Servants of Satan

He said they were "disguising themselves as apostles of Christ." Paul begged the Corinthian Christians, whom he loved dearly, not to yoke themselves together with these unbelieving false apostles. He begged the church to make room in their hearts for him.

Paul's Boasting

You could say, in a way, that the entire letter of 2 Corinthians is Paul boasting about his ministry. However, through the wisdom of God's Spirit, Paul boasted in a way that was entirely different than the way his critics boasted. In the first half of the book, Paul boasted about the triumphal procession in which Christ was leading him; the glory of the gospel that he proclaimed; the power of God that worked through him; and the churches, like Corinth, who were the proof of his apostleship.

Paul had a special ministry, not because he was smart, not because of his resume, not because of his appearance, not because of his talent or ability. Paul had a special ministry because Jesus commissioned and empowered him. So when Paul boasted of his ministry, he made it clear, his sufficiency was from God, who made him sufficient to be a minister of a new covenant.

In the second half of the letter, when Paul was being more direct, he even used the word "boast." But his boasting centered around what he had suffered for Jesus. He did not boast in his strength, but in his weakness. He boasted in the fact that he was constantly persecuted and plagued by a "thorn in the flesh." However, in all of his suffering, he was sustained by the all-sufficient grace of God.

In light of the cross, it isn't oratory skills or an impressive appearance that proves a person is a servant of Jesus. In the light of the cross, the proof is suffering. And Paul had plenty of suffering to prove he had taken up his cross and was truly following Jesus.

Paul's Impending Visit

There seems to be a thinly veiled threat throughout the letter. Paul wanted the church in Corinth to do the right thing, to be the people Jesus called them to be, and to listen to his teaching. According to the good report Paul received from Titus, there was plenty of reason to believe many of the Corinthians were on the right track, but there was also reason to believe some in Corinth needed to experience spiritual discipline.

Paul was afraid when he showed up, he would find, "quarreling, jealousy, anger, hostility, slander, gossip, conceit, and disorder." He was afraid he would find many who sinned earlier had not repented of the "impurity, sexual immorality, and sensuality" they had practiced. He was afraid he would find their promises of financially supporting the church in Jerusalem to be hollow. These fears caused him to delay his personal trip to Corinth and to write this letter warning them about his arrival.

Listen to Paul's stern words in the final chapter:

> *This is the third time I am coming to you. Every charge must be established by the evidence of two or three witnesses. I warned those who sinned before and all the others, and I warn them now while absent, as I did when present on my second visit, that if I come again I will not spare them—since you seek proof that Christ is speaking in me. He is not weak in dealing with you, but is powerful among you. For he was crucified in weakness, but lives by the power of God. For we also are weak in him, but in dealing with you we will live with him by the power of God.*

Paul had King Jesus' authority to "not spare" the disobedient if he showed up and still found them to be rebellious. Even though he did not want to deal with them harshly, he had the power and the authority to do so. I do not know exactly what this threat means, but no doubt the rebellious would have been kicked out of the church if Paul showed up and they were still continuing in sin.

Devotion to the Apostles' Teaching

In all of this, Christians today should remember that our faith is built on the teaching and testimony of the apostles. If we desire to be followers of Jesus, we cannot treat the writings of Paul (or any other apostle) as optional. Jesus was speaking through Paul when he wrote these letters.

This is why I get very frustrated when Christians today put more weight and emphasis on the gospel accounts (Matthew, Mark, Luke, and John) than they do on the epistles. Matthew's testimony about Jesus is not more authoritative than Paul's. The words Jesus spoke in the flesh are not more important than the words Jesus spoke through his apostle Paul. That's what "apostleship" is all about. These men were all hand-picked ambassadors of King Jesus.

We must devote ourselves to the writings of all the apostles if we wish to understand our King and follow him in a way that pleases and glorifies him.

GALATIANS

The book of Galatians might be the earliest of Paul's epistles and it is definitely the harshest. When this letter was written to the churches in Galatia, Paul was steaming mad with righteous anger because false teachers were corrupting the churches he planted on his first missionary journey.

Distorting the Gospel

Paul dealt with a particular problem throughout his ministry: Jewish Christians who insisted that Gentile Christians should be circumcised and keep the Law of Moses in order to be considered part of the community of faith. In Galatia, it seems there were some Jewish church leaders who gave into this way of thinking primarily out of fear. Paul said they started teaching this idea "in order that they may not be persecuted for the cross of Christ."

These Jewish church leaders knew they could escape persecution if they were to say to their Jewish persecutors, *No, we aren't part of that radical group of Jesus followers. We are not fraternizing with uncircumcised people. These Gentiles we eat with are converts to Judaism. They have been circumcised and they keep the Law.*

Out of fear, these Jewish Christians taught their Gentile brethren, *It's great that you believe in our Messiah, but now you also need to be circumcised and keep the Law. But if you remain uncircumcised, then I can't even eat with you.* They taught that the Law was the true basis for a right relationship with God and circumcision was still the sign that a person was part of the covenant people of God.

Paul called the ideas being spread in Galatia a different, distorted, and contrary gospel.

Now, let me clear on something. It is not fair or accurate to call every teaching with which you disagree a "distortion of the gospel" or a "different gospel." If someone has different views on some things, it doesn't necessarily mean he or she has "fallen from grace" or believed "another gospel." In fact, it seems to me that a lot of folks accuse others of distorting the gospel when they themselves often have very little understanding about what the gospel really says.

The Gospel

What is the gospel? Most of us probably know that gospel means "good news." But "good news" about what? What is the good news? What has "the cross of Christ" really accomplished? We really ought to learn to think and speak within the categories laid out in books like Galatians.

If there is one phrase in Galatians that defines the gospel it would be this, "Jesus Christ...gave himself for our sins to deliver us from the present evil age, according to the will of our God and Father, to whom be the glory forever and ever." And there is another phrase that Paul actually says is the gospel being preached to Abraham, "In you shall all the nations be blessed."

The gospel is not a set of rules. The gospel is not a new law from God. The gospel is that Jesus has given himself to deliver people of all nations from the present evil age and secure for them the inheritance God promised to Abraham. That is the gospel. So, the next logical question is, "Who are the people being delivered from the present evil age and who will inherit these blessings?"

Heirs of the Promises

Christians today tend to ask very different questions than the questions actually being addressed in Scripture. We ask questions like, *What do I need to do to make sure I get to go to heaven?* Do you notice how that doesn't sound anything like what Paul addresses in this (or any) letter? Paul isn't addressing how to go to heaven, he is addressing who are the heirs of the promises God made to Abraham.

Do you remember the story we started all the way back in Genesis? We haven't switched stories. The Bible hasn't suddenly changed storylines on us. It hasn't suddenly become a story about floating on a cloud for eternity.

GALATIANS

What Paul wrote in Galatians is that Gentiles who have given their faithful loyalty to King Jesus have become descendants of Abraham, heirs of the promises God made to their father Abraham. Paul writes:

> *For as many of you as were baptized into Christ have put on Christ. There is neither Jew nor Greek, there is neither slave nor free, there is no male and female, for you are all one in Christ Jesus. And if you are Christ's, then you are Abraham's offspring, heirs according to promise.*

A Gentile woman, a slave boy, a pious Jew, a Gentile landowner, Jesus has given himself to deliver all of these people from the present evil age and make them heirs according to promise. It would be hard for a Jew to accept, but Paul really did claim that through Jesus, every believer in Jesus could consider himself or herself a descendant of Abraham.

The Spirit

Paul also made the point that the presence of God's Spirit within their lives is the evidence that uncircumcised Christians really are full-fledged members of the covenant community of God. In other words, circumcision is not the sign of belonging to God, the sign is the presence of the Holy Spirit. And he emphatically reminded them that the Spirit, and not the flesh, needs to be their concern.

Some of the people in Galatia were concerned with whether or not a man's "flesh" had been cut away, but they needed to be concerned with whether or not a man was full of, "love, joy, peace, patience, kindness, goodness, faithfulness, gentleness, and self-control." These qualities are from the Spirit. This is the fruit the Spirit of God produces in a person's life when he or she walks by the Spirit instead of by the flesh.

It seems to me, Christians today walk by the flesh when we are overly concerned about the appearance of things rather than the work of the Spirit in our lives. Like the Galatians, we also need to walk by the Spirit and not by the flesh. We need to learn not to put yokes of slavery on one another. We need to learn to embrace our identity as Abraham's children, indwelt by the Holy Spirit, delivered from the present evil age, and awaiting our inheritance from "the Jerusalem above" to which we belong.

EPHESIANS

In the book of Ephesians, Paul emphasized (as he always seemed to do) that the Gospel of Jesus Christ was not a new idea. Everything Jesus accomplished was part of God's plan since "before the foundation of the world." But there was one thing that was surprising about the Gospel, one thing that had been a secret or a "mystery" before, but now was revealed by the Gospel. What was that "mystery"? What had God's people not expected the Messiah to bring about? What was surprising about the Gospel?

What Do You Think the Mystery Is?

I've always assumed the mystery was something like this: Prior to Jesus, the Jews expected a physical kingdom. They thought the Messiah would come and give them the land back (as the prophets actually promised) and the Jews would live happily under the Messiah's reign forever. However, Jesus died and was raised so they could be part of a spiritual kingdom and go up to heaven someday to live with God.

I always thought the mystery was that the Jews were expecting something "physical," but God had in mind something "spiritual." I thought the mystery was that all of the "physical" things in the Old Testament were just pointing forward to "spiritual" things in the New Testament. I tried to read the whole Bible with this sort of typology mentality until I realized I was overcomplicating the story and misreading everything.

So, take just a second and ask yourself: What is the mystery? What is the thing that was hidden from God's people before Jesus came and revealed God's master plan?

The Mystery Revealed

Paul wrote to the Ephesians telling them exactly what the mystery was:

> *When you read this, you can perceive my insight into the mystery of Christ, which was not made known to the sons of men in other generations as it has now been revealed to his holy apostles and prophets by the Spirit. This mystery is that the Gentiles are fellow heirs, members of the same body, and partakers of the promise in Christ Jesus through the gospel.*

Did you read that? The mystery is not that the Jews were hoping for the wrong things. The mystery is not about spiritual versus physical. The mystery is simple, "Gentiles are fellow heirs, members of the same body, and partakers of the promise in Christ Jesus through the gospel."

The mystery that was hidden in previous generations, but came to light in Christ, was that the people of God who would "acquire possession" of the promised inheritance would be made up of both Jews and Gentiles. That is the thing the Jews did not expect. That is the part of God's master plan that was so surprising.

From Death to Life

The first three chapters of Ephesians are spent describing in great detail the glorious blessings that Gentile Christians have received. Paul reminded them that, prior to Christ, they were "dead in their sins and trespasses." Obviously, they were not dead in a medical sense, so we ought to ask ourselves in what sense they were dead.

Many say, as I have unfortunately said, *Paul means they were "spiritually dead."* But as far as I know, the word "spiritually" is never used in Scripture to describe death. A person can be "spiritually alive" when the Spirit of God dwells within them, but there is no place in Scripture that speaks of being "spiritually dead." It is as nonsensical as, "Brightly dark." They are opposite ideas and cannot be paired together in such a way.

Therefore, I think it is better to take Paul's words to mean that before Christ, the Ephesians were "condemned" in their sins. Death had a claim on them. Before Christ, they would have died without any hope of being raised to immortality. They were dead in the same way Adam and Eve died the day they ate the fruit in the Garden of Eden; driven away from the tree of life, condemned to death.

But when the Ephesians put their faith in Jesus and were baptized into him, they were given life. Not life in a metaphorical sense, but literal life. Because of Jesus, death no longer had a claim on them. When Jesus returns, our Ephesian brothers and sisters will be raised to live forever "in the kingdom of Christ and God."

Royalty in Christ

In addition to the language about being dead and now being alive, Paul also uses all kinds of language that makes one think of royalty. These Gentile Christians, by putting their faith in Jesus, had become part of the ruling class. They had been exalted to seats in the "heavenly places" with Jesus. This isn't just part of the future promise, but part of their present reality as Paul is writing them this letter.

Paul described how these Gentiles used to be cut off from God and the promises of Israel. He said they had been hopeless aliens and strangers, but because of "the blood of Christ," they had been reconciled and even exalted. He wrote, "So then you are no longer strangers and aliens, but you are fellow citizens with the saints and members of the household of God."

This royalty language soon gives way to temple language as Paul describes how they are the temple of God where the Holy Spirit dwells.

Walk Worthy of the Calling

The first three chapters set the stage for the final chapters of Ephesians. In chapter four, Paul transitions from, these are the blessings of being part of God's royal family, and transitions to, since you're part of God's royal family, here is how you must live. These Gentiles are actually not Gentiles anymore. They are now part of the new Israel, the new creation, and they must live like it.

Applying Ephesians to our lives, if we want to be part of the new Israel, the new creation, we also must "walk in a manner worthy of the calling to which you have been called." If we are in Christ, we are no longer Gentiles, we are part of God's royal family. We must live like new creation people if we hope to one day "acquire possession" of the inheritance God has promised to his people.

PHILIPPIANS

Paul's letter to the Philippian church is short and sweet. It can very easily be read in one sitting. In fact, with books as short as Philippians, I like to read them twice in one sitting. If you do that, you may just pick up on something you missed the first time. That's exactly what happened to me.

What is Fellowship

Unfortunately, when we think about "fellowship" we typically think about sitting around talking to one another or sharing a meal with each other. Don't get me wrong, sharing a meal together and visiting with each other is an incredibly important part of being a Christian family, but there is far more to real fellowship than that.

The Greek word we translate "fellowship" is "koinonia" and the word meant something like partnership. In the first-century world, to be in fellowship with someone meant to be partners with them in some joint effort. Sharing a meal with someone might have implied to others that two people were in fellowship, but the meal wasn't their fellowship. Their fellowship was a deep and intimate partnership.

Paul's Fellowship with the Philippians

Paul uses the word "koinonia" (and other closely related words) throughout his letter to the Philippians, but it is translated with various English words like partnership, participation, and sharing. For Paul, his fellowship with the

Philippian church was all about the fact that they were partnering with him to share the Good News about Jesus with the world.

They partnered with Paul both in their financial support and in their prayers. Paul very much believed that when someone was praying for him, they were helping his missionary work to succeed. He believed strongly that the prayers of the Philippians would help him get out of prison.

There was nothing in the world more important to the apostle Paul than proclaiming the Good News of Jesus. The people closest to his heart, those for whom he had the most affection, were those who shared that vision. His appreciation boiled over for those who "labored side by side with [him] in the gospel," those he called "fellow workers, whose names are in the book of life."

Paul's love for the church in Philippi wasn't based on how many potlucks they had shared together, but on the fact that they were committed to helping him reach the world with the Good News about Jesus.

Additional Types of Fellowship

Paul also mentioned his fellowship with other partners in the gospel. Specifically, Paul talked about men like Timothy and Epaphroditus. These were men Paul considered "fellow workers" and "fellow soldiers." These were men who had often risked their lives to help Paul spread the Good News.

But there are other "fellowships" mentioned in Philippians. There is a fellowship of the Spirit. Paul encouraged the Philippians to be of one heart and mind based on their "participation in the Spirit." In other words, the Spirit of God was partnering with the church to make them into the people he wanted them to be. The Spirit was working inside of them "to will and to work for his good pleasure," so they could "shine as lights in the world." Paul taught them that this partnership they shared with the Spirit, ought to impact the way they treated one another.

Another "fellowship" in Philippians is a fellowship of suffering. Paul longed to "share" (koinonia) in Christ's suffering. He viewed suffering for Jesus as a way of being in deeper fellowship with Jesus. And when the church sent Paul a gift in prison, he said they were sharing in his trouble. They were in deep fellowship with him when they sacrificed of their own means to try to lift part of his burden.

Having Real Fellowship Today

There is much we can apply from this theme to the church today. Ask yourself some of these questions:

> Are you in fellowship with your church family?
>
> Do you consider yourself their partner, helping them with burdens and struggles, sharing with them the responsibility of reaching your community with the Good News?
>
> Are you in fellowship with preachers, evangelists, and missionaries? Do you partner with them by in sharing your finances and prayers to ensure their success?
>
> Are you in fellowship with the Spirit?
>
> Do you understand that the Spirit of God wants to partner with you to change the way you think, feel, and act?
>
> Are you participating with him so you are a light shining in the world?
>
> Are you in fellowship with Jesus?
>
> Do you long to share his suffering and are you sharing in the suffering of persecuted brethren throughout the world?

Spend some time today reading through Philippians. Spend some time thinking and praying about your fellowship.

COLOSSIANS

The book of Colossians is similar to Ephesians in many ways, but it is also incredibly unique. Colossians can be read in just a few minutes but it may prove to be somewhat challenging to understand. Paul wrote this letter to the church in Colossae to keep them faithful, to inoculate them against false doctrine. I am firmly convinced that the method Paul used for keeping the church faithful still works today.

The Problem in Colossae

It's not hard to pick up on the fact that there must have been some teachers who were teaching the Colossian church false doctrine. There may have even been multiple groups of false teachers, teaching conflicting philosophies, but they all posed a threat to the church.

The false teachers in Colossae seem to have been critical of those who ate certain kinds of foods, drank certain kinds of drinks, failed to observe certain special days. Paul said these false teachers wrongly insisted on things like asceticism and worship of angels. They went on and on about their visions and were puffed up without reason by a "sensuous mind." They were promoting a human philosophy and a self-made religion.

Paul's goal with this letter was to ensure that false teaching (no matter how plausible the arguments) would not be accepted by the church. Paul wanted to make sure his brothers and sisters in Christ would not be disqualified from receiving their inheritance. Paul wanted to make sure that when this church family is someday presented to Jesus they are all mature, holy, blameless, and above reproach.

Preach Jesus

In order to keep the church from being led astray, Paul's strategy was simple...preach Jesus.

We seem to forget sometimes, the thing that should draw people to Christianity is the beauty of Jesus. We don't make disciples by having more convincing philosophies or arguments. We don't make disciples by having more engaging entertainment or church programs. We make disciples by sharing who Jesus is and what he has done. And if that's the reason people become followers of Jesus, then that is also the reason they remain faithful to him.

Knowing this, Paul exalted Jesus. He told the church in Colossae, only in Jesus would they find:

> all the treasures of wisdom and knowledge
>
> spiritual circumcision
>
> resurrection to life
>
> forgiveness of sins
>
> victory over the forces of darkness

Compared to what Jesus has to offer, peddlers of philosophy and self-made religion have absolutely nothing of value.

Preach the Hope of Our Inheritance

Paul also reminded the Colossians about the fact that they have a "hope laid up for [them] in heaven." Notice this is a bit different than telling them their hope was to go to heaven. That's not what he said. He said their hope was being stored in heaven.

What is this hope laid up in heaven? Paul would go on to say it is the "hope of glory." In other words, it is the confident expectation that when Christ appears, they also "will appear with him in glory." Paul calls this the "inheritance of the saints in light." Trying to persuade them to remain faithful to Jesus, Paul reminded them "that from the Lord [they] will receive the inheritance as [their] reward." This is another thing the false teachers could not offer.

COLOSSIANS

The consistent teaching of Jesus and all the apostles is that Christians should not be eagerly anticipating death, but eagerly anticipating Jesus' return. Jesus will bring with him our "glorious inheritance" (Ephesians 1:18) that is currently "laid up in heaven" for us. He will give to us, and to all of God's people, the inheritance that was promised to Abraham and his descendants.

Preach New Creation

As with previous letters, Paul taught the Colossians that becoming a follower of Jesus means becoming a part of a new creation. Because of Jesus' kingly victory over the ruling powers that enslaved us, we have been empowered to become a new kind of human being.

Paul taught the Colossian Christians to put on this new humanity. Allowing their new humanity to be seen in their working relationships, their family relationships, and everything they did or said. The qualities of this new humanity are things like compassion, kindness, humility, meekness, patience, forgiveness, and love.

The power to become this new kind of person does not come from philosophers or teachers of the Law, but from Jesus himself.

Keeping Churches Faithful Today

My big takeaway from Colossians is that if we are going to keep individual Christians and whole congregations faithful, we must simply preach Jesus. Who is Jesus? What did is his death and resurrection accomplish? What sort of inheritance has he promised to bring to his people? What power does he offer us to transform our lives in the present? If we want to persuade people to follow Jesus, these are the types of questions on which we should focus our attention.

THESSALONIANS

Based on what Luke recorded about Thessalonica (see Acts 17), we know there were very few Jews in the city who wanted anything to do with Paul or his gospel. However, he was able to make some headway with "a great many of the devout Greeks and not a few of the leading women." But when Paul started gaining this small following, the Jewish leadership became jealous. Some of the Jews stirred up a mob, broke into a Christian home, and had a few Christians arrested. Eventually, Paul had to slip out of town at night, but some of the trouble-making Jews from Thessalonica hunted Paul down in the next town to make trouble for him there as well.

It broke Paul's heart that he was "torn away" from the small Christian community in Thessalonica before he could really help them reach a state of maturity. He was understandably terrified that the persecution they continued to suffer would cause this little band of Jesus followers to lose heart and fall away. But when Paul's protege Timothy went back to Thessalonica to check on and continue teaching them, it was discovered they were maintaining their loyalty to Jesus in spite of the persecution.

Sanctification

One of the themes I noticed in both first and second Thessalonians is the theme of sanctification. Paul wrote that it was God's will for them to be sanctified. Or, in other words, God wanted them to go through a process of being made holy.

In order to be sanctified, Paul gave instructions to "abstain from sexual immorality." Before coming to Christ, most of these Gentile Christians had engaged in pagan worship rituals and lived lives reflecting the ethics and morals of the Greco-Roman culture. So, adopting the sexual ethic taught in the Hebrew Scriptures would have been quite a shift for many. Paul encouraged them, saying God wanted each of them to "know how to control his own body in holiness and honor, not in the passion of lust like the Gentiles who do not know God."

Paul wrote that it was the presence of the Holy Spirit within them who was causing them to be sanctified. Which is why Paul prayed for God to sanctify them "completely," so their "whole spirit and soul and body" would "be kept blameless at the coming of our Lord Jesus Christ."

I wonder, how often do we pray for the complete sanctifying work of the Spirit in our lives?

Second Coming

It is interesting, as I've noted in previous chapters, the Bible doesn't talk a lot about Christians going to heaven. Yes, of course, there are a handful of passages that (thankfully) tell us our spirits will be perfectly safe with the Lord when our bodies sleep in the grave, but that disembodied state is only temporary and is not the primary focus of any of the apostles' teaching.

The primary hope of the First-Century church, as reflected in both First and Second Thessalonians, is the second coming of King Jesus. When Jesus returns, he will raise those who are "asleep" from the grave and there will be a great reunion with all of his people, both the living and the dead. Paul pictures a scene that is perhaps reminiscent of the "Triumphal Entry," when the crowds met Jesus on the road outside Jerusalem, laid down palm branches, and shouted "Hosanna in the highest!" Similarly, when King Jesus is "revealed from heaven," all of Jesus' followers will meet him in the air to worship him and celebrate his return.

King Jesus' return will mark the end of all evil, violence, oppression, poverty, war, and persecution. There will be no more suffering and no more dying. All of Jesus' enemies will be forever vanquished and his people will be set free from their suffering. On that day, all of the promises of the Scriptures shall be finally and completely be fulfilled in Jesus.

Because of his reign, prophecies like Isaiah's will be fulfilled (Isaiah 11:6, 9):

> *The wolf shall dwell with the lamb, and the leopard shall lie down with the young goat, and the calf and the lion and the fattened calf together; and a little*

child shall lead them…for the earth shall be full of the knowledge of the Lord as the waters cover the sea.

Suffering

As Christians wait for the return of King Jesus, we must understand we are "destined" to "suffer affliction." In the First Century, as well as today, the meek suffer ridicule and persecution. In these two letters alone, Christians are called to be at peace, repay no one evil for evil, always seek to do good to everyone, abstain from every form of evil.

This Jesus-like lifestyle will appeal to some; they will find the radical love of Jesus followers irresistible. But this lifestyle will also intimidate and infuriate others. As in earlier days, people will assume we are traitors or conspirators because we love our enemies and refuse to do evil even to those who do evil to us and others. People will hurl insults at us, question our allegiance, and wonder if we can be trusted.

But our loyalty and allegiance are to our King and to his kingdom. We know that any "light momentary affliction" we must endure will prepare "for us an eternal weight of glory beyond all comparison" (2 Corinthians 4:17). So we seek to live a "peaceful and quiet life, godly and dignified in every way" (1 Timothy 2:2), as we wait for King Jesus to return and set all things right.

TIMOTHY & TITUS

Paul's three short letters to his sons in the faith, Timothy and Titus, might be compared to a coach's locker room speech or a commanding officer trying to inspire his troops. In these three letters, Paul describes the type of work these young ministers ought to be doing.

The Minister's "Charge"

One of the recurring words, especially in Paul's letters to Timothy, is the word "charge." Paul had "charged" both of these young ministers to do a job. He had entrusted them with great responsibility. Timothy had been sent to work with the Ephesus church and Titus with various churches on the island of Crete. Like soldiers sent on a mission, these were their marching orders.

Be A Teacher

The primary area of responsibility on which Paul told Timothy and Titus to focus was teaching. Both communities with which these men were working were plagued with false teachers. So the church in both communities needed men who would devote themselves "to the public reading of Scripture, to exhortation, to teaching."

Paul encourages these men to teach the women, the men, the young, and the old. He wants them to teach the people about Jesus and the grace of God. He wants them to teach people how to live the kind of lives that are consistent with faith in Jesus. Here is the sort of thing Paul tells Titus to declare:

> *For the grace of God has appeared, bringing salvation for all people, training us to renounce ungodliness and worldly passions, and to live self-controlled, upright, and godly lives in the present age, waiting for our blessed hope, the appearing of the glory of our great God and Savior Jesus Christ, who gave himself for us to redeem us from all lawlessness and to purify for himself a people for his own possession who are zealous for good works.*

The church continues to need men who will be devoted to teaching and reminding Christians how to live in a way that is consistent with faith in Jesus.

Be A Leader

I find it undeniably true that Timothy and Titus were entrusted with positions of leadership. Paul gave marching orders to these two men and they were expected to turn around and command, charge, and entrust various responsibilities to other Christians in their local communities.

In other words, Timothy and Titus were given the job of delegating. They were not expected to do all the teaching, correcting, or ministry themselves. They were told to pass these responsibilities on to elders, deacons, and other "faithful" disciples of Jesus. There was a sort of delegated authority Paul had, a delegated authority these ministers had, and a delegated authority the elders, deacons, and others had when the baton was passed to them.

When we seek to learn from this example, perhaps the most important question isn't, "What is the chain of command in the church?" We get so caught up in church politics, but maybe some better questions would be things like:

> Is everyone busy serving the Lord?
>
> Is the church being shepherded?
>
> Is the truth being taught?
>
> Are people loving and serving one another?

If the answer to these questions is "yes," then maybe we shouldn't worry too much about the pecking order. If the answer is "no," then someone needs to be charged with some responsibility. Pass the baton to a faithful person and encourage them to do what needs to be done.

A Model of Good Works

One of the most important parts of both Timothy and Titus' roles was modeling good works. If Timothy and Titus taught the truth about Jesus, but their life did not reflect the Spirit's sanctifying work, then their teaching would be in vain. This, of course, does not mean Timothy and Titus had to be perfect, but it does mean teaching and preaching always brings a level of scrutiny for which these men needed to be prepared.

These are the sort of instructions Paul gave to them: Pursue righteousness, faith, love, and peace; avoid controversies and quarreling; be kind to everyone; patiently endure evil; correct opponents with gentleness. I love what Paul wrote to Timothy,

> *The aim of our charge is love that issues from a pure heart and a good conscience and a sincere faith.*

The goal of everything Paul was doing was love. Love that issues from a pure heart. Paul knew that in order for his own ministry to be successful and for the ministries of his proteges to be successful, they had to all model love and work to bring about love in their life of the church.

Ministers in Today's Church

Whether we are talking about preaching ministers, involvement ministers, missionaries, or youth ministers, if a person has devoted their lives to the gospel, then there is much to learn from Paul's letters to Timothy and Titus.

They should primarily focus on teaching. They should find and dispel the myths and correct the misunderstandings we all have in our minds. They should explain to us, from the Scriptures, what lives look like that are consistent with the Good News of Jesus. They should be theologians, saturating their hearts and minds in Scripture so they can teach others.

They should also lead and be empowered to lead. They should delegate responsibilities and equip others to minister alongside them in the kingdom. They should not be seen as hired hands, but as fellow soldiers in our battle against the schemes of the devil.

And finally, they should set examples of love and good works. And of course, when they stumble, they should find grace and forgiveness, being allowed (and even expected) to confess sins and struggles (just like any other Christian). If we do not extend grace and forgiveness to our ministers, we will continue to have festering sin hidden below the surface; which will eventually be exposed and destroy lives, ministries, and the reputation of the church.

May we all continue to build one another up, understanding that "the aim of our charge is love."

PHILEMON

Although the book of Philemon is a very short letter, it can be challenging to understand because it deals with slavery. Christians in the United States have a difficult time conceiving of slavery apart from the type of slavery that existed in the United States until the 1860s. Even though the slavery of first-century Rome was quite different, there is much that followers of Jesus in every time and culture can learn from this letter.

A Word About Slavery

I have written in the past about the evils of slavery, particularly the type of slavery that existed in the United States. The enslavement of African men, women, and children continued in American territories for over 270 years and has only been abolished for about 150 years. This evil has shaped our culture more than many of us would like to admit.

Horrifyingly, there are also many forms of slavery that exist around the world today. It is estimated that there are around 40 million people who live in some form of slavery today. Thankfully, most modern Christians are rightly outraged by the slavery of the past and the present.

When reading Paul's letter to Philemon, we might wonder, why doesn't Paul condemn slavery outright? Why doesn't Paul rebuke Philemon for taking part in the evils of slavery? If you think it is because Paul doesn't believe slavery is wrong, you need to read the letter again. I truly believe if the heart of this letter had been accepted by all those Europeans who claimed to be followers of Jesus, the African slave trade would have never existed!

PHILEMON

Voluntary Goodness

Many years ago, when I first read Paul's letter to Philemon, I read it as being sort of a passive-aggressive letter. Paul obviously wanted Philemon to love and forgive Onesimus and accept him back into his household as a brother. But Paul stopped short of commanding Philemon to do the right thing, saying, "I am bold enough in Christ to command you to do what is required, yet for love's sake I prefer to appeal to you."

It's easy to read Paul's words, "I prefer to appeal to you" and "confident of your obedience" as being less than sincere. It's easy to think Paul isn't really confident Philemon will do the right thing. However, I choose to believe Paul is incredibly sincere and is exceedingly confident that Philemon will do the right thing.

Paul is explicit about why he wrote this letter as an appeal instead of as a command. It wasn't because Paul didn't have the right to command Philemon. It wasn't because Philemon was free to do anything he wanted to do in this situation. The right course of action was clear and anything less than that would certainly have been sinful and wicked. However, Paul did not want to rob Philemon of the opportunity to do good voluntarily. Paul said he wrote the way he did, "that your goodness might not be by compulsion but of your own accord."

This is a consistent theme throughout Paul's letters, Paul wants followers of Jesus to voluntarily do good and be a blessing to others. Even though it is a Christian's obligation to do so, Paul doesn't want people to do good out of compulsion. He wants Christians to do what is right because they want to do it. He never wants to steal from someone the opportunity to choose the right path.

Transformed Relationships

I believe the most important theme of this letter is that faith in Jesus transforms relationships. Because of their shared faith in Jesus, Onesimus has been caring for Paul like a son would care for his aging father. And when Onesimus returns to the household from which he fled, the expectation is that he will no longer be treated as a slave, but will now be a family member.

My favorite line is this, "Receive him as you would receive me." Can you imagine how that would play out if it were truly obeyed? Onesimus was a runaway slave and Paul expects the Gospel of Jesus Christ to so transform his former master that he will receive Onesimus in the exact same way he would receive the apostle Paul.

PHILEMON

What might Philemon had done to receive Paul? Prepare a room for him, wash his feet, serve a feast in his honor, listen attentively to stories of his travels. In other words, Philemon would serve Paul, because that's what a follower of Jesus is supposed to do. Followers of Jesus consider others to be more significant than themselves and serve them selflessly (Philippians 2:1-5). Paul expected Philemon to do the same for Onesimus, serve him as he would serve any other honored guest in his home.

And Onesiums, who at one time could not wait to get away from Philemon's house, was returning to serve. He wasn't returning to serve as a slave but returning to serve as a brother in Christ. What a beautiful picture: a former master and a former slave, now mutually submitting to one another and serving one another; each treating the other as if his brother was "more significant" than himself.

Charge That to My Account

Finally, I must say a word about Paul's willingness to pay Onesimus' debts. Paul wrote to Philemon:

> *If [Onesimus] has wronged you at all, or owes you anything, charge that to my account. I, Paul, write this with my own hand: I will repay it.*

While making a sincere offer to pay any outstanding debt, he fully expected Philemon would probably refuse to accept Paul's money because he himself felt indebted to Paul.

This is what it looks like to follow the example of Jesus. Going to the cross, Jesus paid our debts in order to bring about reconciliation. Jesus was willing to say, on behalf of all those enslaved to sin, "Charge that to my account." He did this to reconcile heaven and earth, bringing God and humanity back together.

Jesus' act of selfless love also brings about humanity's reconciliation with each other. When we become followers of Jesus, we begin looking for opportunities to bring people together, even if we have to say, "Charge that to my account." When two parties are at odds with one another, we seek to bring them together, even if the results of their misdeeds have to fall on us.

Now that we are no longer slaves, we seek to free others from slavery. We seek to bring about peace and reconciliation in the world, even when we must follow in our Savior's footsteps and have another's debt charged to our account.

HEBREWS

The book of Hebrews is an amazing book. The Hebrew writer, whoever he may have been, helps his audience understand the continuity between (what we now call) the Old and New Testaments. He helps his Jewish audience understand that following Jesus is, in a sense, a continuation of their temple worship, but also why following Jesus is superior to temple worship.

The Audience

I might be wrong, but it seems that Hebrews may have been written to Christians living in Jerusalem. The author reminds them of when they were first enlightened. He said they endured a hard struggle with sufferings, were publicly exposed to reproach and affliction, had compassion on those in prison, and joyfully accepted the plundering of their property. This sounds a lot like the "great persecution against the church in Jerusalem" (Acts 8:1), when Saul of Tarsus was "ravaging the church, and entering house after house, he dragged off men and women and committed them to prison" (Acts 8:3). Now, decades later, they are receiving this letter because remaining faithful to Jesus is especially difficult in Jerusalem.

Imagine being a Jew, living in the shadow of the glorious temple, and trying to follow Jesus. Your patriotism, heritage, and faith would be so intertwined with that building and all of the rituals and ceremonies performed in that building. It would be so hard to walk away from all of that. It would be so hard to live with the shame of feeling you had abandoned the traditions of your family.

HEBREWS

For many Christians, the pressure probably became too great and they started abandoning the church community in favor of the temple, the priesthood, the sacrifices, and the city of Jerusalem; the things they could see. The writer of Hebrews desperately pleads with Christians not to neglect the Christian assembly or lose faith in Jesus.

Following Jesus is More Jewish

When speaking to a Jewish audience, the apostles had one goal: help Jewish people realize that following Jesus is the most Jewish thing they could do. If first-century Jews wanted to be faithful to the God of their ancestors, then they should be disciples of Jesus. Being a disciple wasn't a break from the faith of their ancestors, but a faithful continuation of their ancestral heritage. And what was true then is still true today - Christianity isn't a separate religion from Judaism; it is the true form of Judaism.

The Hebrew writer reminds his audience that being a disciple of Jesus doesn't mean they have rejected the prophets, the Law delivered by angels, Moses, the temple, the priesthood, or the sacrifices. Following Jesus didn't mean rejecting any of those things, because Jesus is the one to whom all of those things point and Jesus brings about a reality of which those things were but mere shadows.

The challenge was that the temple, the sacrifices, and the priests could all be seen, but the reality Jesus brought was "yet unseen." This is why the Hebrew writer explains that the Jewish faith has always been a matter of "assurance of things hoped for" and "conviction of things not seen." By following Jesus, the High Priest they could not see, who made atonement in the temple they could not see, waiting for the city they could not see, they were living like Noah, Abraham, Moses, Joshua and countless other ancestors who had come before.

Heaven and Earth

Modern Christians have a tendency to talk about things that are "spiritual" and things that are "physical." This is really a false dichotomy and it's not the point biblical writers are trying to make. We might be tempted to put the things the Hebrew writer discusses in terms of "spiritual" and "physical," but those aren't even the terms used in the book of Hebrews.

The Hebrew writer isn't contrasting spiritual and physical things, but heavenly and earthly things. He wants his audience to understand that the things that are right now "unseen" are no less real than the things are "seen." In fact, there is a sense in which they can be even more real, because they will always endure; they are "unshakable" because they are heavenly.

One day those heavenly realities, that are right now invisible, will become visible. What is unseen will one day be seen. We live now in anticipation of that Day, convinced that the things of the unseen realm are the true and unshakable realities.

The World and City to Come

When the book of Hebrews was written, Jerusalem may have seemed like the center of the Universe. It may have seemed like the unshakeable city, the city where David reigned, the city of the temple, the most important city in the world to a Hebrew man or woman. But it was a city that would soon fall.

The writer of Hebrews wanted his audience to understand that they may be kicked out of the Jerusalem "camp," but that was ok,

> *Jesus also suffered outside the gate in order to sanctify the people through his own blood. Therefore let us go to him outside the camp and bear the reproach he endured. For here we have no lasting city, but we seek the city that is to come.*

Jerusalem was not the true city of God, but there is a "city of the living God." There is a "city that has foundations, whose designer and builder is God." There is a "heavenly Jerusalem." This city is the one the Hebrew writer encouraged his readers to "seek." This is the "city that is to come" in the "world to come."

Someday, all those who lived their lives seeing the unseen, will receive the promises for which we have waited. We will "rise again to a better life" and the city that has foundations built by God, the heavenly Jerusalem, will come and we will be with God forever.

JAMES

The book of James might be one of the easiest books for Christians to understand, regardless of time and culture. It deals with the sort of issues and behaviors that are common to religious people of every era, and there is really no misunderstanding what James is telling his audience to do and not to do.

The Audience

James simply addresses this book to, "the twelve tribes in the Dispersion." This could mean he is writing to Jewish Christians, or he could be referring to all Christians as part of the new Israel. The book doesn't seem to be a letter intended for a specific church. In fact, it doesn't really seem to be a letter at all, because there is no formal greeting in the beginning or the end.

James seems to be writing to the kind of Christians who think very highly of themselves; the kind of people who consider themselves to be wise, religious, and capable teachers. They are critical and judgmental. They want to live comfortable lives. They envy wealth and scorn poverty. They believe themselves to have a lot of faith and a lot of wisdom, but what they really have is a lot of words.

Be Quiet and Listen

It's interesting to me how often James' words, "Be quick to hear, slow to speak, slow to anger" are taken out of context. People typically quote these words as a strategy for interpersonal relationships. They say things like,

"God gave us two ears and one mouth, so we should always do twice as much listening as we do talking." Certainly, it's good advice to listen more than you talk, but James has a specific kind of listening in mind.

In the same context, James writes, "put away all filthiness and rampant wickedness and receive with meekness the implanted word, which is able to save your souls." Too often, when someone is trying to share a word which is able to save our souls, we get angry and defensive. James tells his audience to "receive with meekness the implanted word." It is almost always a good idea to be quiet and listen, but especially when someone is trying to correct our "filthiness" and "wickedness."

How often do we get defensive when someone shares the word of truth with us? How often do we get angry at those who are trying to help us? How often do we say, "I disagree," when we ought to say, "You might be right, let me think about that"?

Faith, Religion, and Wisdom Can Be Seen

James touches on various issues throughout this short book, but they all seem to revolve around the idea that it is not enough to say we are religious people, people of faith, or people with wisdom. We must prove our faith, religion, and wisdom by what we do. Words do not prove what is in our hearts, action proves what is in our hearts.

James tells his audience to "be doers of the word, and not hearers only." He tells them that real religion is about helping widows and orphans. He tells them faith without works is as useless as wishing someone well who has no clothes or food.

To those who think they are wise, James says that their "bitter jealousy and selfish ambition" prove their wisdom is "earthly, unspiritual, demonic." Real wisdom isn't about the ability to conjure up the right words to put opponents in their place. Real wisdom is proven by good conduct and meekness. Real wisdom, wisdom from God, is: pure, peaceable, gentle, open to reason, full of mercy, full of good fruits, impartial, and sincere.

In all of these areas, James invites his readers to prove they are wise, religious, and faithful by living lives of humble and loving service to others.

Poverty and Suffering

Like his brother Jesus, James warns about the dangers of comfort and wealth. He encourages his audience to be content with poverty and trials. The book begins by encouraging people to, "Count it all joy," when they,

JAMES

"meet trials of various kinds." He promises that patiently enduring trials will result in being, "perfect and complete, lacking in nothing."

He warns them not to give preference to rich people over poor people who visit their assemblies. He implies that riches do not make someone admirable, reminding that the rich are the ones who "oppress you," the ones who "drag you into court," and the ones who "blaspheme the honorable name by which you were called."

James includes one of the strongest warnings and condemnations of those who live their lives in self-indulgence, taking advantage of others:

> *Come now, you rich, weep and howl for the miseries that are coming upon you. Your riches have rotted and your garments are moth-eaten. Your gold and silver have corroded, and their corrosion will be evidence against you and will eat your flesh like fire. You have laid up treasure in the last days. Behold, the wages of the laborers who mowed your fields, which you kept back by fraud, are crying out against you, and the cries of the harvesters have reached the ears of the Lord of hosts. You have lived on the earth in luxury and in self-indulgence. You have fattened your hearts in a day of slaughter. You have condemned and murdered the righteous person. He does not resist you.*

James closes the book by encouraging his readers to think of themselves as farmers. As farmers wait patiently for the harvest, Christians wait patiently, "for the coming of the Lord." We live our lives not based on what we can see, but in confident expectation about what is to come.

1 PETER

Like most of the books in the New Testament, 1 Peter can be read in a matter of minutes. When you read it in one sitting, I recommend reading it two or three times in that same sitting. This is one of those books that challenges a lot of our American ways of thinking. What would our lives look like if we really took the whole book of 1 Peter seriously?

Your Time of Exile

Peter calls his audience "exiles of the Dispersion." This idea typically referred to Israelite people who were scattered throughout various nations after the Assyrian and Babylonian Empires conquered and exiled them. Even the Jews who came back to Jerusalem were, in a sense, still exiles because a foreign empire ruled over them and occupied their nation. Being an exile wasn't just about where you were living, but about the state in which you were living.

According to 1 Peter, all Christians have become part of the "Dispersion." We are all exiles, waiting for our exile to be lifted and for all of us to be gathered together to receive our inheritance. But it is very important to note that Peter doesn't talk about us receiving our inheritance by flying away to heaven. He seems to assume we will receive our inheritance by the things in heaven coming to us.

Peter never uses words that indicate we will GO anywhere when our exile is ended. He uses words like "appear" and "reveal." Our faith will "result in praise and glory and honor at the revelation of Jesus Christ." Our inheritance that is guarded in heaven will be "revealed in the last time." When Jesus "appears," we will "receive the unfading crown of glory." We will rejoice and be glad when Christ's "glory is revealed."

Like the Hebrew writer, Peter seems to picture Jesus, heaven, and our inheritance as things that are now hidden or unseen, but one day they will appear, become visible, be revealed. According to Peter, it does not seem Christians should be waiting to "go to heaven," but that we should be waiting for the heavenly things to appear. This is when our exile will be over, when the "chief Shepherd appears" and gathers his dispersed sheep.

Responding to Mistreatment

The vast majority of this book deals with how Christians should respond when they suffer mistreatment. Modern readers, especially those in the United States, seem to have a very difficult time taking these commands seriously. We try to insert our own caveats, creating excuses for why we shouldn't have to obey the instructions Peter gives to his audience.

There are no caveats. There is no nuance. No matter what sort of mistreatment a Christian is suffering, Peter tells them to respond the way Jesus responded:

> *When he was reviled, he did not revile in return; when he suffered, he did not threaten, but continued entrusting himself to him who judges justly.*

That is the simple and undeniable message of 1 Peter, do not respond in kind to those who revile and mistreat you. But it even goes beyond just not retaliating. Peter writes:

> *Do not repay evil for evil or reviling for reviling, but on the contrary, bless, for to this you were called, that you may obtain a blessing.*

Peter tells his audience to "bless" (speak and do good to) those who do evil to them. Why should we be surprised that 1 Peter is a book about doing good to persecutors and not responding violently to those who mistreat us? The entire New Testament preaches this message without fail.

This is the message of the cross. This is how Christians are to join with Jesus in overcoming evil: when we are mistreated we bless those who do evil to us, hate us, revile us, and even kill us. I admit, this isn't very American. It certainly isn't John Wayne or Clint Eastwood. It's Jesus. This is what it looks like to follow Jesus.

The Word of God

Almost as a side note, we need to be very careful when we read the phrase, "word of God" and mentally replace it with, "the Bible." Those two phrases "word of God" and "the Bible" are related, but not synonymous. When the biblical authors are talking about the "Scriptures," they will say they are talking about the "Scriptures." But when they are talking about the "word of God," they are talking about something far more specific than all of the Scriptures.

Peter tells his audience they have been born again through the "imperishable seed" of the word of God. Peter references Isaiah 40:6-8:

> *All flesh is grass, and all its beauty is like the flower of the field. The grass withers, the flower fades...but the word of our God will stand forever.*

In other words, God always delivers on his word. Peter is telling his audience that even though they are suffering right now, they can take confidence in the fact that they will be rescued from their suffering because God has spoken.

So when you read "word of God" or "word of the Lord," don't generalize those phrases by interpreting them to mean "Bible" or "Scriptures." Understand that "the word of God" is something very specific, a promise or command that proceeds from God and accomplishes his will in the world.

Saved by Baptism

When Peter tells his audience that baptism is now saving them, what does this have to do with his overall theme of, *You're suffering right now as exiles, but because you have been born again by the imperishable word of God, you should have confident hope?*

When we pull one verse out of context that says baptism saves us, we might think it means we are forgiven of our sins because of baptism. It is true that we are forgiven when we are baptized, but that's true because other passages say it (Acts 2; Romans 6), not because this passage says it.

In this passage, Peter seems to have a slightly different emphasis. He tells his audience they are being saved right now by the water of baptism the same way Noah and his family were saved by the waters of the flood. From what was Noah saved? Following the logic of Peter's argument, Noah suffered mistreatment by disobedient people, "while the ark was being prepared." The water of the flood came and saved Noah from those disobedient people.

In the same way, mistreated and suffering Christians can take heart that their rescue has already begun. The waters of baptism are now saving us. The waters of baptism separate those of us who are being saved, from those who are rejecting the message of Jesus. So we can confidently and peacefully live with mistreatment because we are being rescued from this life of suffering and our new life will soon be revealed.

2 PETER

There are many who believe it is impossible for someone to be saved and then fall away. They believe that if a person becomes a Christian and then falls away, they were never really saved in the first place. However, I'm not sure how you could maintain a belief in "once saved, always saved" after sitting down to read 2 Peter. From start to finish, this is a letter warning Christians about falling away.

False Teachers

Peter's big fear is that after he has died, the disciples he taught would be drawn away by false teachers. Peter not only describes the condemnation of such false teachers, but also the sorts of things they were teaching. Their false teaching was marked by things such as greed, sensuality, blasphemy, and boastfulness.

Not only were these false teachers bound for condemnation, but those they led astray would likewise be condemned. Peter warned anyone who abandoned a life of following Jesus in favor of this kind of sensual lifestyle would be punished by God on the day of judgment.

Peter makes it clear that he is not talking about people who were never saved. He is talking about people who had "escaped the defilements of the world through the knowledge of our Lord and Savior Jesus Christ," but are "again entangled in them and overcome." Peter says that if a person is delivered from sin and then entangled in sin again, "the last state has become worse for them than the first."

These false teachers promise freedom, but their teaching results in themselves and their hearers being enslaved to their passions.

Standing Firm

But just because it is possible to fall away and suffer condemnation, does not mean most will suffer that fate. It is possible to focus so much attention on Peter's warning about falling away that we completely miss his hope that his readers will stand firm.

Peter tells his audience they will always remain in a right relationship with God if they are diligent to increase in qualities like faith, virtue, knowledge, self-control, steadfastness, godliness, brotherly affection, and love.

He certainly doesn't give them the impression they could *accidentally* fall away from God at any moment. Falling away is what happens to Christians who stop resisting and struggling with sin and just totally give themselves over to their appetites. Peter assures them if they practice things like self-control, brotherly kindness, love, etc. they will "never fall."

The Day of the Lord

In the midst of his warnings about what will happen to the wicked and ungodly, Peter describes what might be called the destruction of the world. At first glance, it might seem Peter is contradicting Jesus who says the meek will inherit the earth (Matthew 5:5) and Paul who says the descendants of Abraham will inherit the world (Romans 4:13). Peter, on the other hand, talks about things being burned with fire. However, I certainly do not believe Peter is contradicting Jesus, Paul, or the Old Testament prophets (who promised the earth would be filled with the knowledge and the glory of God).

To understand Peter's argument, you have to understand he is saying that this world we live in now is not the first world to exist; there was a world that existed before this world. However, "the world that then existed was deluged with water and perished." Obviously, the fact that the pre-flood world "perished," does not mean it was annihilated from existence. It means that after the flood, the whole world was different, changed, and transformed. That old world was gone and a new world took its place.

Peter says the world that exists now is awaiting a similar event to the flood. The earth will be judged and will no longer exist as it does now, but nothing in the text necessitates the understanding that the earth will be annihilated from existence.

Peter seems to be saying that the sky (the "heavens") is like a veil that separates the visible world from the invisible world, but on the "day of the Lord," that veil will be dissolved with fire and all of the evil deeds people are doing on the earth will be exposed to the light of God's judgment. We might think of it like a giant curtain being torn away so the One who is behind the curtain can come through and deal with everything on this side.

New Heavens and New Earth

Peter says that after "the day of the Lord," the righteous will receive a "new heavens and a new earth." This is the moment for which we are all waiting. In this new creation, Peter says, "righteousness dwells." After the ungodly and all of their works are destroyed, the only thing left will be righteousness.

The things Peter wrote here, of course, are right in line with everything Jesus, the other apostles, and the prophets have said about the resurrection and the "age to come." Peter isn't saying the physical universe will cease to exist and we will all live in some non-physical realm. There isn't even a hint of such a thing in his words. He simply says the world after the day of the Lord will be "new" in the same way the world after the flood was "new."

I believe the new heavens and new earth will be a changed and transformed version of the old in the same way our resurrection bodies will be a changed and transformed version of the old. In Romans 8, Paul said the creation itself will "be set free from its bondage to corruption and obtain the freedom of the glory of the children of God" (Romans 8:21). The creation will no longer be subject to decay or corruption. Like our mortal bodies, the creation will be redeemed (Romans 8:23).

This is our hope. This is our confident expectation. The evil and wickedness that carry on day-after-day will not always exist. Justice will be served and God's people will be rescued. God only delays so that even more people might be saved.

JOHN'S EPISTLES

John's epistles are a great example of why context, following an author's train of thought, and appreciating an author's unique style are so incredibly important. John assumes his audience can see the beautiful themes he has expertly woven into the fabric of the text. Therefore, we run the risk of completely misunderstanding any single verse when we rip it from its context to use it as an isolated prooftext.

The Gospel of John

The resemblance in themes between John's gospel account and the epistles of John is striking. He continually explores the ideas of light, life, love, and truth. As I read several times through 1 John, I couldn't help but feel there was a circular pattern to the book. The ideas of light, life, love, and truth continued to swirl around and around in concentric circles. And in the short books of 2 and 3 John, these themes are apparent as well.

For John, these themes are intimately connected. Jesus is the light of the world that has broken into a world of darkness and is transforming his people into light-bearers by giving them life, love, and truth. This light is continuing to grow and will someday fill the whole world. The darkness will be completely dispelled and there will eventually be nothing but light in the world.

In a practical sense, when we are people of truth and love, we participate with God in being light and dispelling darkness. John writes:

> *The darkness is passing away and the true light is already shining. Whoever says he is in the light and hates his brother is still in darkness. Whoever loves his brother abides in the light, and in him there is no cause for stumbling.*

Therefore, reading 1, 2, and 3 John serves a great introduction to John's gospel account. By reading these short epistles, you can see that in his gospel account John is not just giving a historical biography on Jesus, but is giving a robust theological treatise on what it means for Jesus, the Son of Man, to be reigning with God as King.

A World of Stark Contrast

In John's epistles, he presents things in stark contrast. There is very little nuance or gray area. Everything is either: Light or Dark; Truth or Error; Love or Hate; God or the Devil.

This doesn't mean nuance doesn't exist or that there are no gray areas in life or theology; it simply means that in John's context, there was a pressing need to draw stark contrast between those who were in the light and those who were in the darkness. He was dealing with false prophets, people who were denying essential truth about Jesus, but were trying to pass themselves off as genuine followers of Jesus. So, apparently, lines had to be drawn in the sand to differentiate between those who were true followers of Jesus and those who were not.

For John, it is "evident who are the children of God, and who are the children of the devil: whoever does not practice righteousness is not of God, nor is the one who does not love his brother." For John, the primary line of demarkation was love for fellow Christians. For John, if someone believed in the name of Jesus Christ and loved his brother, they were obeying the commandments of Christ and were God's children. If they did not believe and love, then they were in the darkness and were children of the devil.

I think it's important to realize that there is a time for nuance and a time for stark contrast; followers of Jesus need to understand which is which. When we are having a conversation about the particulars of the Christian faith, we must understand we are likely having a nuanced conversation.

Don't treat your brother, who disagrees with you on some matter of Christian faith or practice, as someone who is "in the darkness." Just because someone disagrees with you about how things ought to happen in the Sunday assembly, for instance, does not mean that person is not abiding "in the teaching of Christ" or that he "does not have God." But also, don't be dismissive of conversations and debates that are trying to work out the particulars of Christian faith and practice. These conversations are not the sort of conversations John was having, but they are still important.

Changing the World Through Love

All of the themes, ideas, and concepts that John explores are important, but there is no theme more important than love. John depicts the people who truly love others as being possessors of light and life. When you love like Jesus loves, you show the world a new way of being human and this new humanity will live forever with Jesus. John writes, "We know that we have passed out of death into life, because we love the brothers. Whoever does not love abides in death."

For John, love means taking care of one another. It means seeing someone in need and meeting their needs. He implores his readers, "Little children, let us not love in word or talk but in deed and in truth." John believes if someone refuses to meet his brother's needs when he has the ability to meet them, he hates his brother and should not consider himself part of the community of light.

Following Jesus means making Jesus' death our way of life, "He laid down his life for us, and we ought to lay down our lives for the brothers." Love is selfless. Love is sacrificial. Love serves.

Love is the new way to live. It's actually the only way to live. Selfishness and hate are the way to die, but selfless love is the way to live now and forever. This is the way we participate with Jesus in bringing light to this world of darkness.

JUDE

There is so much packed into the tiny book of Jude. The way Jude turns a phrase is beautiful and almost poetic. But because of the subject matter, it is certainly not pleasant. Jude references many events from biblical literature and even some events from literature outside of the biblical canon, all to warn his audience that God will judge the ungodly. This is a subject modern Christians probably need to consider a little more often.

Contend for the Faith

Jude told his audience that his goal for writing this book was to appeal to them to "contend earnestly for the faith that was once delivered to the saints." That is an important phrase and one we should all take seriously, but it is also a phrase we must let the text define. What does it mean to "contend earnestly for the faith"? We must read Jude's letter to understand.

According to Jude, contending for the faith seems to mean "building yourselves up in your most holy faith" in order to "keep yourselves in the love of God, waiting for the mercy of our Lord Jesus Christ that leads to eternal life." In other words, contending for the faith means, first and foremost, remaining faithful to Jesus and building up other Christians so they remain faithful.

Jude is afraid his audience will fall prey to the wicked false teachers who "have crept in unnoticed" and show up at the church's "love feasts" and feast with them "without fear." For Jude, contending for the faith seems to be a battle that is less about offense and more defense. He wants his audience to be aware of these false teachers and be on guard against their schemes.

Another aspect of contending for the faith is to "have mercy" on those who are having doubts or are struggling with sin. Though much of Jude's letter focuses on wicked people who will face the judgment of God, the vast majority of people with whom we come into contact are not wicked people. They are not false teachers who need to be sharply rebuked. Most people we meet in our lives are those on whom we simply need to "have mercy."

Contending for the faith isn't about being a watchdog or about beating people over the head. It's about keeping yourself committed to Jesus and having mercy on others.

Perverting Grace

The only time Jude uses the word "grace" in the entire letter is when he writes about the false teachers "who pervert the grace of our God into sensuality." The false teachers about whom Jude was warning obviously considered themselves followers of Jesus and recipients of God's grace, but their lifestyle was one of selfish indulgence and ungodly speech. Jude pulls no punches when he says these people will face God's judgment.

Jude wants his audience to understand these false teachers who promote this type of behavior are perverting the gift of God and will face severe judgment and condemnation. Jude reminds them of people and events like:

> Korah's rebellion
>
> Balaam
>
> Sodom and Gomorrah
>
> Disobedient angels

All of these, in one way or another, squandered the gifts of God, pursued their own desires, and were destroyed.

I feel this subject is incredibly relevant for modern Christians. There seems to be a multitude of false teachers today, "who pervert the grace of our God into sensuality." They seem to teach that what God wants most is for people to be happy, following their own dreams. In doing so, they excuse behavior like drunkenness, sexual immorality, marital unfaithfulness, and more.

We should heed the warnings of this little book and not be drawn away by false teaching.

Having the Holy Spirit

Another area that I think needs to be drawn out of the text of Jude is his emphasis on the Holy Spirit. He describes the false teachers as people who are "devoid of the Spirit." I think sometimes we fail to understand that it is impossible to live a Christian life without the Spirit of God dwelling in us. The apostle Paul wrote in Romans 8:9-11,

> *Anyone who does not have the Spirit of Christ does not belong to him. But if Christ is in you, although the body is dead because of sin, the Spirit is life because of righteousness. If the Spirit of him who raised Jesus from the dead dwells in you, he who raised Christ Jesus from the dead will also give life to your mortal bodies through his Spirit who dwells in you.*

Christians are supposed to be like a new version of humanity, a Spirit-empowered version of humanity. It's like we have the old hardware (our bodies), but we have received upgraded software (the Spirit) in anticipation of the final hardware upgrade (our new bodies in the Resurrection). As we live our lives, we must walk according to the Spirit of God who lives within us and empowers us. The Christian life is a Spirit-empowered life, but those who live according to the flesh are, "devoid of the Spirit."

Also, notice that Jude tells his audience to be "praying in the Holy Spirit." Christians are supposed to intentionally rely on the power of the Holy Spirit when we pray. After all, Paul also wrote that the Spirit helps us when we pray. The Holy Spirit is willing to participate with Christians in prayer, but apparently, we must be intentional about relying on his help, support, and power while we pray.

I am not talking about speaking in tongues or picking up deadly snakes and I don't think that's what Jude has in mind either. This type of Spirit-empowered life is marked by the fruit Paul describes in Galatians 5, "love, joy, peace, patience, kindness, goodness, faithfulness, gentleness, and self-control." These are the signs that a human being is walking and praying in the Spirit. Let's focus on being Spirit-empowered people who are contending earnestly for the faith.

REVELATION

It is a shame that the book of Revelation is either ignored or read in a hyper-literal way. Christians seem to either be scared of it or obsessed with trying to "decode" it. I think we should simply heed the admonition at the beginning of the book by reading it aloud, hearing it, and keeping the things that are written in it. Revelation blessed its original audience and it can continue to bless the church today if we will heed its encouraging and timeless message.

Apocalyptic Literature

When reading Revelation, we should notice the similarities with other books in the Bible that use similar types of images, symbols, and metaphors to convey their messages; books like Daniel and Ezekiel. Apocalyptic literature pulls back the cosmic curtain and allows us to see what is going on behind the veil. As humans, we naturally see wars, famine, death, and persecution, but apocalyptic literature allows us to see that there are actually spiritual forces at work, both evil and good. Apocalyptic literature is meant to give hope to God's people in the midst of horrible situations.

It helps to understand the symbolism; like understanding that a beast represents a world empire or a horn on that beast represents a king or ruler. However, even if you don't understand the specific symbols, you can still grasp the big picture of the book. And with books like Revelation, the big picture is the most important part. If you get bogged down in any of the fine details, you will likely miss the whole point.

REVELATION

The main point of this book is that the Lord is in charge of the world, is working to bring about his will on the earth, and will ultimately be victorious over all the forces of evil. And because these things are true, God's people should be faithful and not afraid.

The Seven Churches

Many of us have probably spent a lot of time reading and thinking about the specific messages Jesus gives to the seven churches in Asia. We tend to like these messages because they seem practical and not dependent on the rest of the book. However, there is much about these messages that a reader might miss by not finishing Revelation.

For instance, in the messages to the seven churches, Jesus constantly describes the future blessings and inheritance of those who remain faithful and loyal to him. This inheritance is hinted at all throughout the book, and then in the wonderfully climactic scene, the inheritance is revealed and received. Jesus promises those who conquer, things like this:

> They will not be hurt by the second death.
>
> They will receive the hidden manna, and a white stone.
>
> They will receive authority to rule with Jesus over the nations.
>
> They will be clothed with white garments.
>
> They will have an important place in the temple of God in the New Jerusalem.
>
> They will sit with Jesus on his throne.

These promises to the faithful, that they will live and reign with Jesus, run like a thread throughout the book. One of the dominant themes of the book is this, if you are faithful to King Jesus, you will be one day be glorified and will reign with him. The Lamb is praised:

> *You were slain, and by your blood you ransomed people for God from every tribe and language and people and nation, and you have made them a kingdom and priests to our God, and they shall reign on the earth.*

So, when you read the messages to the churches in Asia, be sure to note the descriptions of Jesus, the warnings to those in rebellion, and the promises to the faithful. All of these ideas and images are expounded upon throughout the rest of the book.

REVELATION

Beasts and Babylons

Sadly, Christians have spent the last 2,000 years arguing about how the book of Revelation should be interpreted, "Which kings do these ten horns represent?" Or, "Who is the beast or the harlot?" Certainly, I believe John had specific cities, empires, kings, and people in mind when he used apocalyptic language to figuratively describe them in this book. These kingdoms and rulers existed in his day and his audience would no doubt have understood to whom he was referring.

However, the book of Revelation isn't linear. It isn't written to be followed like a chronological timeline of events. Revelation is cyclical. It describes cycles of evil empires and nations rising up, and when their wickedness is complete, having the wrath of God poured out on them.

If the prophets and apostles had wanted to simply say specifically, *Such and such nation will fall*, they could have said that. However, they gave us something far more valuable. These apocalyptic books help us to understand that at any given moment, there is far more going on in the world than meets the eye. There is a spiritual war between good and evil waging in the world. Countless beasts and Babylons have risen up (and will continue to rise up), but when their wickedness is complete, Jesus brings judgment upon them.

In the midst of wars and conflict upon the earth, God's people are continually reminded about the one "who is, who was, and who is to come."

The Great Wedding Day

There is absolutely no better way for our Bibles to close than with this great climactic scene at the end of Revelation. Our Bibles began with the forces of darkness leading humanity astray and the world coming under a great curse, but our Bibles end with that curse being completely undone.

The last couple of chapters of Revelation are all about the final destruction of all evil, wickedness, and even death itself. God's rescue plan, that he carried about in Jesus, will finally be complete when heaven and earth are joined together. The final moments of John's vision are like a wedding, the place of God and the place of man reunited, reconciled, brought together in perfect harmony.

That's the story of the Bible, if you haven't picked up on it in the previous chapters, Jesus is rescuing us so that when the city of God comes down out of heaven and is joined like a bride to the earth, we will have access to the tree of life and will live forever in the presence of God. This is the "new heavens and new earth" that the prophets and apostles promised. In that place and time, "death shall be no more, neither shall there be mourning, nor crying, nor pain anymore, for the former things have passed away."

Because we believe these things, we say, "Come, Lord Jesus!"

Made in the USA
Monee, IL
15 April 2020